# CREATIVE
## GLASS
*painting*

# CREATIVE
## GLASS
# *painting*

## Moira Neal

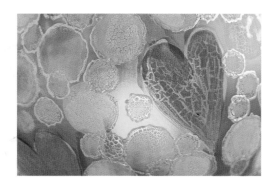

David & Charles

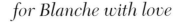

*for Blanche with love*

A DAVID & CHARLES BOOK

First published in the UK in 2002
by David & Charles
ISBN 0 7153 1212 X (hardback)

Distributed in North America
by F&W Publications, Inc.
4700 E. Galbraith Rd.
Cincinnati, OH 45236
1-800-289-0963
ISBN 0 7153 1267 7 (paperback)

COMMISSIONING EDITOR *Lindsay Porter*
ART DIRECTION *Ali Myer*
DESK EDITOR *Jennifer Proverbs*
STEP PHOTOGRAPHY *Tony Neal*
STYLED PHOTOGRAPHY *Amanda Heywood*

Printed in Hong Kong by Dai Nippon
for David & Charles
Brunel House, Newton Abbot, Devon

www.moiraneal.com

# CONTENTS

# Introduction

Nothing excites me more than filling my house with all the paraphernalia required to write a book, to experiment and come up with lots of new ideas.

Glass painting has developed rapidly during the past decade and there are many exciting new products on the market now. They are readily available, offer much scope to enthusiasts, and some also allow glassware to be cleaned in a dishwasher without coming to any harm. Glass paints may be purchased in bottles, in felt-tipped pens or as outliner in a tube. Some are water soluble and only suitable for decorating ornamental pieces, others are solvent based and more durable. I have used the Pébéo range of paints for the projects in this book, and paints of the same brand name and type can be blended together to produce an almost endless array of colours.

Writing this book was particularly exciting as a new product, peel-off glass paints, had recently come onto the market. Aimed mainly at the under-ten age group, this product appealed to the child within and I had to have a go with it. Soon my workroom window was full of my attempts and I realized that there was far more to this product than meets the eye. If it peels off glass and can be repositioned, then it must be the perfect substance for making stencils. Wow! Soon every jam jar in the house played host to

my research and I became more and more excited by the possibilities of this invention. As you turn the pages of this book, you too will see just how useful it can be and the different ways in which it may be used.

The projects I have created here are attractive, useful and simple to achieve. You do not need to be an artist to produce stunning results. Patterns and templates have been provided but I am sure most of you will be confident to re-create the designs freehand. The projects are fully described in steps, with clear photographs. There are also useful sections on the basic tools and materials required and the techniques used.

My advice is to experiment and have fun and use the ideas to help you to design your own unique pieces of designer glassware. Just remember, you don't need to be 'artistic' to be creative and creativity doesn't have to be difficult.

# GETTING STARTED

*Whether you are new to glass painting or are already hooked, you will find*

*everything you need to know in this chapter about creating items similar to the*

*ones in this book. As all the projects are very much technique-based, you will find*

*easy-to-follow instructions for all the methods used to decorate the glassware.*

*There is also advice on the basic tools and materials you will need.*

You can either produce the projects exactly as they are in the book, or extract bits from each to create your own designs. Be free with colours, experiment endlessly and practise on every unpainted piece of glassware you can get your hands on!

# GLASSWARE

*The shops are full of the most imaginative glassware and mirrors,*

*with lots of items suitable for decorating. You may not be able to buy exactly*

*the same styles as we have used in the book but the designs and ideas may*

*be adapted to suit your choice of glass.*

As glass painting can be a great recycling hobby, hunt around car-boot sales, jumble sales and flea markets for items suitable for decorating. Avoid any glass that is broken or damaged. It's best not to decorate antique glassware you may have come across, in case you devalue it. If you find interesting glassware at a sale, make sure you can remove any stains before taking the time to decorate it, as the stain may obscure the decoration. Second-hand glass is usually very cheap but once decorated in an original way it makes a great present. Even a number of dissimilar glasses may be united simply by using a cohesive colour scheme to link them. This is particularly useful if you are having a large party, as your guests are more likely to remember which glass is theirs. Better still, they may even place an order for you to paint a unique collection for them too!

The shops are full of plain glassware just waiting to be transformed using the excellent selection of glass painting materials available

# TOOLS AND MATERIALS

*The tools and materials needed for glass painting are very simple and the basics are described below. I'm sure once you get hooked you will find your own favourites to use.*

To save excessive repetition in the project materials lists, you will find it useful to have some basic tools and materials to hand. These should include drawing pens and pencils, coloured pencils, a selection of felt-tipped pens, sharp scissors, scalpel or craft knife, cutting mat, metal ruler, scrap paper, tracing paper, masking tape, adhesive tape, paper glue, spray glue, white spirit, cotton buds, cocktail sticks, paper towel, clothes pegs, a variety of paintbrushes, sponges, cling film (Siran wrap) and some old plates for mixing paint.

## GLASS PAINTS

There are a great many types of glass paint available nowadays, with immense fun to be had experimenting with them all. I hope to share some new and novel glass painting ideas with you within the pages of this book.

The glass paints I've generally used are the Virea 160 range by Pébéo (see Suppliers) which have to be oven baked at 60°C for forty minutes to fix them. Pébéo also do another range called Porcelaine 150 which are for glass or ceramic items. These also have to be baked and come in clear and opaque colours. You could of course use paints and products from

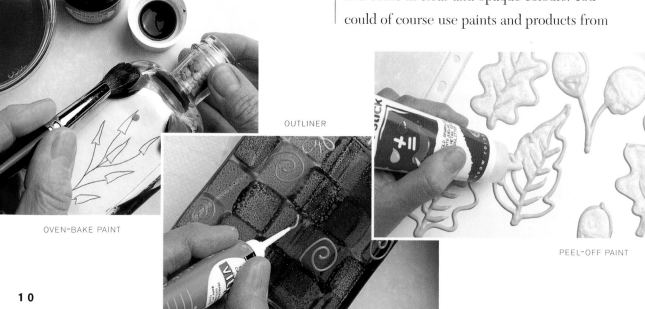

OVEN-BAKE PAINT

OUTLINER

PEEL-OFF PAINT

other manufacturers but the shades will vary from those shown in the photographs here.

The glass paints used in this book include air-drying paints, oven-bake paints and peel-off paints. They may be applied to the surface of glass in a variety of ways and these are described in Techniques beginning on page 15.

**AIR-DRYING PAINTS:** The air-drying paints used in this book are ceramic paints and are solvent based. They are *not* suitable for children to use and great care must be taken when handling them as they are difficult to remove from clothing. Brushes and sponges used on ceramic paints will need to be cleaned with white spirit. The advantage of these paints is their density of colour and although they are not dishwasher proof, they are fine for painting decorative items. Solvent-based, clear glass paints are also available and are particularly useful for marbling onto glass as they float on water. They are also wonderful for recreating a stained-glass look on decorative items such as lanterns and candle holders. Also available in craft shops are water-based, air-drying paints. As with all glass paints, make sure you use them in conjunction with compatible outliners.

**OVEN-BAKE PAINTS:** The beauty of these paints is their suitability for use on tableware and the fact that they are dishwasher resistant. There are oven-bake paints made especially for glassware but you can also use oven-bake ceramic paints on glassware too if you wish. Do make sure that you leave pieces that have been decorated with outliner to dry for *several* days before baking as this will reduce the chance of the outliner bubbling and spoiling your work.

**PEEL-OFF PAINTS:** As mentioned in the introduction, these paints are a wonderful new product. They are such great fun that I got totally addicted, my view of the fields clouding with the number of peel-offs on my window! It was then that I had the idea to use the stuff for making re-usable stencils. I tried grids and stars, leaves and hearts. I got too impatient and tried to peel the masks off too soon, with the result that the whole lot stuck to itself and it was another twenty-four hours before the replacement was ready to be used. However, all my play has resulted in a new way of using the product and the results are within these pages for you to share (see Techniques page 18). After much hard work, I've ironed out the wrinkles, so you can use the method with confidence!

## OUTLINERS

Outliner is thick glass paint in a tube and is used for outlining areas of glass paint, for adding details to a design or as a paint in its own right to create patterns from dots, lines or swirls. There are a number of colours available including gold and silver, and they may be oven baked or air dried. Make sure that you choose an outliner that is compatible with the paint you have chosen.

## PAINTING PENS

Felt-tipped paint pens are very simple to use and are available in either gloss or frosted finish. A wonderful etched effect can be created by using a colourless, frosted pen. Children find felt paint pens particularly easy to use and they are not messy. As the paints dry very quickly, the designs may be baked almost immediately and children are soon able to enjoy using their decorated glassware to eat and drink from, or to give as gifts.

## GEL

This product, Crystal Gel, comes in a tube and dries to resemble textured glass. It may be applied using a spatula or brush and is available in an exciting range of colours, both clear and opaque or glittery. The gel is thick enough to support objects being embedded in it, such as the foils used in the foil mirror project. Other items that may be embedded include glass nuggets, finely coiled wire, coins, netting, sequins and buttons. It may also be etched into.

PAINTING PEN

## FROSTING SPRAY

Frosting spray mimics a frosted-glass effect and enables you to achieve very quick, professional results although it does not produce a permanent, washable effect so is best used for decorative items only. Aerosol paint is perfect for decorative items such as mirrors and vases.

## DILUENT

This is a thinning medium which can be used to dilute any of the Pébéo Vitrea 160 range without affecting their colour or resistance.

## GLOSS MEDIUM

This is one of a range of mediums available for glass painting. It may be used alone to create a contrasting smooth pattern on a piece of frosted glass, or with a gelled item such as that used on the foil mirror project. Alternatively, it may be

SPARKLY GEL

PAINTBRUSH

mixed with gloss glass paints, the paint retaining its brilliant gloss finish.

Other mediums are available including frosting or matt medium, which may be used alone to produce an etched-glass effect or be mixed with other colours from the same range to produce a frosted effect. Iridescent medium may also be used either alone or mixed with other colours from the same range to produce iridescent effects.

## DRAWING GUM

This product is particularly useful for masking off areas of glass in order to resist the paint, as in the dragonfly tank project on page 44. Fine details are possible if you use a fine paintbrush. Allow the product to dry before painting over it. Wash brushes immediately in soapy water to remove all traces of the product or your brushes will be spoilt.

DRAWING GUM

## ANTI-ADHERENT

This product may be used in conjunction with Crystal Gel. It is painted on the surface of the glass and allowed to dry. Any gel applied over the top of the anti-adherent is then easily removed. This is particularly useful if you want to create jewellery, or shapes that need to be re-applied, as on the foil mirror project on page 32. You may not always find it necessary to use anti-adherent as the gel may sometimes be peeled off if you carefully prise up one edge of it using a scalpel.

## PAINTBRUSHES

The most obvious method of applying glass paint is to use a brush. There are many different types of paintbrush in a multitude of sizes, so it is worth experimenting with them. Seek out fan brushes, long, thin sign-writer's brushes, wide flat brushes and angled brushes – all may be used to obtain different effects. Sponge brushes are also available and are fun to use. See Techniques page 16 for suggestions.

## COTTON BUDS

Cotton buds are cheap and easy to obtain and may be used to apply paint in several ways, such as spotting and stippling (see Techniques page 17). They are also useful for removing areas of unwanted paint or outliner. Cotton buds come in various sizes and shapes according to the manufacturer, so allowing you to experiment with different sizes.

## SPONGES

Sponging is always very successful with glass paints and it is easy to create your own shapes. A coarse, open sponge creates a rustic pattern as long as the paint is not applied too heavily. A fine sponge will create a far more uniform, delicate effect. It is worth experimenting with all different kinds of sponge, from the ones sold for washing dishes (wash thoroughly first to remove any detergent) to cosmetic and bath sponges, torn into small, useful pieces.

## STAMPS

Stamping is yet another way to work with glass paint. There is now an exciting range of stamps available, or you can produce your own from potatoes for rustic effects, or from a commercial heat-impressed foam which is available in a variety of shapes and sizes (see Techniques page 17).

## COLOUR TOOL BOX

This is a great gadget that has been produced for the very popular hobby of stamping. It consists of a handle and clip-on foam tips that come in a variety of shapes. The soft white foam works particularly well on glass and colours may be built up over one another for very interesting designs. Try mosaic effects, patchwork, interlocking patterns and bunches

STENCIL

SPONGE DOT APPLICATOR

SPONGE

of grapes or cherries. Use the white sponge pads for random background patterns and use outliner for added details.

## STENCILS

Stencils have a wonderful range of uses in glass painting and can be used to mask areas off and to apply a design. The range of stencils available is limitless, particularly if you make your own. They can be made from various materials, including paper and self-adhesive plastic (see Techniques page 18).

# TECHNIQUES

*The basic techniques of glass painting are very straightforward and are described here for quick reference. The projects are explained with step-by-step, illustrated instructions, with a list of the specific tools and materials you will need.*

## USING PATTERNS AND TEMPLATES

At the back of the book, beginning on page 116, there is a section called Patterns and Templates, which contains the motifs needed for the projects. Produced actual size, you only need to trace or photocopy the motifs and use them as described in the project instructions. A propelling pencil or sharp HB pencil is best for drawing. Use a ruler and set square so that straight lines are straight and right angles are accurate. The patterns may be enlarged or reduced on a photocopier if you wish.

## MASKING OFF

My tried and tested methods of masking off areas of glass are described here.

**USING MASKING TAPE:** This is available in a variety of widths and may be applied in lines, grids or cut into squares. It is useful for creating geometric patterns too. Try laying a length of tape on a cutting mat and then cut a curved, flowing line down the centre of it. You will then be able to stick the tape onto the glassware back to back to provide a double-sided curved line, as in the set of tall glasses.

Curved masking tape is available and is perfect to mask off flowing, curved lines. It can be used when brushing or sponging on colour. If you want a meandering edge to the curved line, place the tape on a cutting board and use a sharp scalpel to cut the design on one edge.

**USING PAPER MASKS:** Cut or torn paper may be stuck on glass with spray glue to mask off an area or shape and is particularly useful for large designs. The technique has been used in the set of oil bottles. When the paper mask is removed, any trace of glue on the glass may be removed with white spirit.

MASKING WITH TAPE

## APPLYING GLASS PAINTS

Glass paints can be applied in any number of ways. The methods required for the projects in this book include using paintbrushes, sponges, stamps and cotton buds.

**USING A BRUSH:** The most obvious method of applying glass paint is to use a paintbrush. There are many different types in a multitude of sizes, so it is worth experimenting with them to find out what you can do with each one.

Sponge brushes are also available and are versatile and fun to use. Try painting simple square blocks. Pour out the paint onto a saucer or similar and load the brush evenly with the paint, then drag it across the glass to achieve a sharp-edged square. Use the tip of the brush to make straight, narrow lines and patterns.

Combine them with more squares and lines in different colours too. Try the really wide brushes on larger projects, such as mirrors, picture frames and windows. This method is perfect to obscure a window and create a colourful pattern too.

**USING A SPONGE:** Sponging is always very successful with glass paints. Pour out some paint onto a saucer and dip the sponge into the paint. Wipe off any excess on the edge of the saucer before sponging onto the glass. A coarse, open sponge creates a rustic pattern as long as the paint is not applied too heavily. A fine sponge will create a far more uniform, delicate effect, particularly if you keep working over the area to make the paint even. For detailed sponging of small areas, a sponge dot applicator can be used

APPLYING GLASS PAINTS

USING A SPONGE IN CONJUNCTION
WITH A PEEL-OFF STENCIL

(available commercially), or you could make your own from a tiny piece of foam wired onto a cocktail stick or toothpick.

If you want to make a tartan or checked design that is not too precise, try using a foam roller brush. Pour some glass paint onto a tile or other flat surface and then work the roller into the paint to coat it evenly. Roll the paint over the glass surface until it has reached the required density. Allow the paint to dry before using overlays of contrasting paints.

**USING A STAMP:** Stamping is another way to work with glass paint. Cut your own potato stamps for rustic effects or use one of the many commercial varieties available. Make sure you wash out the paint thoroughly as soon as you have finished using stamps. One of the most exciting ways of producing a unique stamp is with heat-impressed foam, which is available in a variety of shapes and sizes from craft shops (see also Suppliers). The foam may be used over and over again simply by re-heating it according to the manufacturer's instructions. It is then pressed into any solid object – from a button or coin to a scattering of rice, seeds, pasta numbers, shapes or letters, or any other object you can think of. Have a trial printing and if you do not like the result, wash, re-heat and re-impress.

**USING A COTTON BUD:** Cotton buds may be used to apply glass paint in several ways. Shake the paint and then use the lid to dip the cotton bud into, and then create simple spot patterns, applying the dots singly or in groups of two or three. Cotton buds can be used to create a

USING A BRUSH

USING A COTTON BUD

stippled pattern too; simply load up with plenty of paint and then stipple onto the surface, distributing the paint evenly. Another way of using cotton buds is to use them to draw lines of paint; this produces an interesting effect, as the edges are more deeply coloured than the centre. Additionally, when the lines overlap each other, a second pattern is created.

APPLYING AN OUTLINER

USING A SELF-ADHESIVE
PLASTIC STENCIL

## APPLYING OUTLINER

Outliner, thick glass paint in a tube, is used for outlining areas of glass paint, for adding details to a design or as a paint in its own right. The technique of applying it is actually quite simple and is similar to icing a cake. Use a steady hand and keep some paper towel handy for catching any blobs on the nozzle. Cotton buds are also useful for lifting off any mistakes.

## USING PLASTIC STENCILS

These are varied and versatile, and have the combined effect of masking off areas *and* allowing a design to be applied.

Self-adhesive plastic stencil film may be cut with fine scissors or a scalpel or sharp knife on a cutting mat. It is paper backed and the design may be drawn or traced directly onto the backing paper before being cut out. Once cut out, place the stencil onto the glassware, pressing down firmly to exclude air bubbles and stop paint seeping under the edges. If you cut out shapes very accurately, you will have positive and negative designs, both of which may be used for different effects.

## USING PEEL-OFF GLASS PAINTS

Peel-off glass paints may be used in an exciting number of ways but primarily they have been designed for decorating windows and other shiny surfaces. Peel-off paints are available as outliners and as paints, and normally the outliner is applied first and then the spaces are filled in with the paints. Peel-off window motifs can be made in the same way as making a peel-off, washable stencil (described opposite) and they may be peeled off and repositioned again and again.

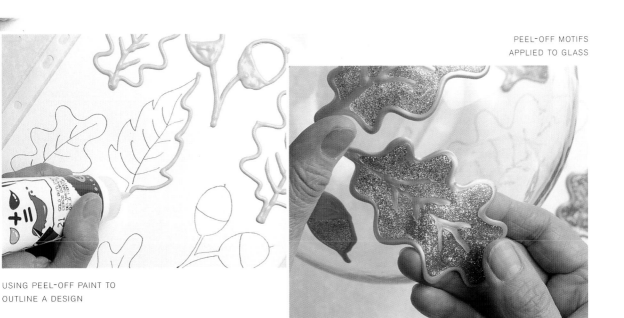

USING PEEL-OFF PAINT TO
OUTLINE A DESIGN

You will need to have a little patience when working with peel-off paints. They need adequate drying time because if you try to remove the shapes too soon, you may end up with a sticky mess! It is best to prepare the decals on a movable, level surface such as a tray, which can be moved well out of the way of prying fingers or paws for a full twenty-four hours, or more if the room is very cold.

Once made, the shapes may be stored on a jar or on the side of a clear A4 pocket. A sheet of stiff card placed inside the pocket will keep the surface firm and flat and allow the designs to be stored safely in a ring binder.

## MAKING A PEEL-OFF, WASHABLE STENCIL

Peel-off, reusable stencils can be created using peel-off glass paints as follows. Start by making a paper template to fit your glassware, then draw the pattern required on this template. Lay a sheet of plastic film over the top of the template (or put the template into a clear, A4 plastic pocket) and squeeze out the glass painting product, following the pattern outlines. Leave to dry for twenty-four hours before peeling off and using the stencil.

A sheet of glass or mirror may also be used as a base on which to make a peel-off stencil. Use some furniture polish on the glassware first to make it easier to remove the stencil. To avoid the stencil getting tangled as you remove it, transfer it as you go onto a cold jam jar or sheet of glass or marble. The coldness makes the product firmer and much easier to handle. Wash the stencil using cold water and a small piece of sponge. The stencil can be washed and reused over and over again.

## USING CRACKLE GLAZE

Crackle glaze is a paint medium that reproduces a cracked, aged look that works very well on glass. The product used in this book is a Pébéo two-part one called Crackling Medium. Phase one is painted on first and allowed to dry. Coloured glass paint is applied over the top and left to dry before phase two is applied. As the glaze dries it shrinks to create the crackled look. I have experimented with the technique and come up with a novel way of using the glaze, as you will see in the crackle-glazed bowl.

One word of warning: do not use crackle glaze in conjunction with stencil film or peel-off glass paints as they both pull off the crackle effect. Instead, paint your design freehand, or copy from a design behind the glass.

## ETCHING GLASS

If you are seeking to achieve a totally permanent result, glass-etching paste is available but no projects in the book use it. It is an extremely caustic product so if you do choose to use it precautions *must* be taken. Worktops, clothing, hands and eyes must be protected and children and pets kept well out of the way.

Oven-bake frosting paints are a far safer and easier-to-use alternative and may be sponged on in conjunction with a stencil. For quick, and non-permanent, results simply use frosting spray. All sorts of designs may be etched into coloured glass paint while it is still wet by using specially designed rubber-tipped shaper tools. You can also use cotton buds, cocktail sticks, fingers or a pencil.

USING A COTTON BUD
TO ETCH A DESIGN

CRACKLE GLAZE EFFECT

BRUSH PAINTING ON A TURNTABLE

## TURNTABLE PAINTING

Record player painting, turntable art, spun designs – call it what you want – are great fun to do. All you need is an old record player turntable. The most basic designs may be simple bands of colour applied whilst holding the brush in one position as the glass item rotates. Further bands of colour may be added in the same or different colours. Band widths may be varied according to the width of the brush used. Practise a clean lift-off with the brush when the band is complete. Further designs may be added by working into the fresh paint. Try using a cotton bud held in one position – this will etch a single perfect circle as long as the plate is centralized before you start!

Turntable painting can also achieve spiral designs. Start with the cotton bud in the centre of

PRODUCING A
BANDED PATTERN

the plate and then slowly bring it towards you – the more slowly you move the cotton bud, the tighter the spiral will be. Try running the turntable at different speeds so you can experiment. You can also push the cotton bud backwards and forwards on the band of colour directly in front of you, which will give an interesting twisted spiral design. Be confident and firm for best results. Just remember that it is easy to simply wash off the paint and start again if you need to.

Running the turntable slowly once the paint is applied can make the basis of another interesting design. Hold the cotton bud in front of you and make tiny circular movements with it. If you are lucky this will result in a triangular design which will grow in complexity the longer you do it. If you move the cotton bud towards you very slowly at the same time, the pattern will grow – experiment! Once you have mastered these basic movements it is time to move on to combining turntable art with stencilled and outlined designs.

The beauty of this spun art technique is that it may be done on the back of a plate or on the outside of a bowl, on areas that do not come into contact with food or with implements which may scratch the surface. It means that the design will be durable but you must learn to think in reverse as you decorate. If you want a stencilled centre, it must be painted first before building up the colour behind it.

# DAZZLING
## *decorations*

Some people are so difficult to buy presents for, but a handmade

gift is always acceptable – just imagine giving the beautiful biscuit

barrel filled with home-baked biscuits. There is also the added bonus

that you will enjoy painting the glass and it will have cost little

more than your time. You may already have a few pieces of

glassware at home to decorate, similar to the ones used here.

Although the collection of projects in this chapter includes

several ideas that would make perfect presents, they are all interesting

to complete as they feature different techniques and glass paints,

including peel-off window paints, gels and

no-bake ceramic glass paints.

# SET OF
## CANDLE
# *holders*

This versatile glassware can be used

as a set of tea-light holders or in a

variety of other ways. For example,

they make a perfect set of vases, or

use them as a desk tidy or for serving

breadsticks and nibbles at a party. If

you wish to retain their versatility, they

need to be decorated in such a way

that they look good no matter what

they are used for.

# Get ready...

SET OF FOUR CANDLE
HOLDERS/VASES
(SEE SUPPLIERS)

OVEN-BAKE GLASS PAINTS
(GLOSS) IN EARTH BROWN,

SANDALWOOD GREEN,
CRIMSON AND PAPRIKA

COMPATIBLE OVEN-BAKE
OUTLINER IN ORANGE
AND GOLD

COMMERCIAL STAMPING
TOOL WITH SQUARE TIP
(OR MAKE YOUR OWN
FROM 2CM/¾IN FOAM)

PAINTBRUSH

# Go!

**1** Pour a little of the first colour onto a mixing plate and dip the stamp into it, wiping off the excess paint. Stamp it onto the glassware using the photograph (or your own painted grid) as a guide.

**TIP**

If you have a foam stamp for each colour you can work more quickly across the glassware alternating the colours as you go.

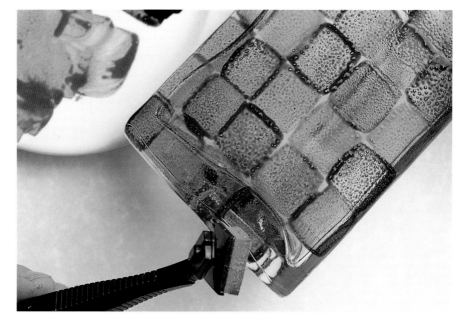

**2** Clean the stamp with water and dry it thoroughly before adding the next colour (see Tip box). Continue as before, filling in the spaces as shown, then do the same with the other two colours. Leave the glassware to dry for about twenty-four hours.

# Get set...

It is a good idea to have a dummy run with the colour combination of your choice before embarking on your project. Simply draw a grid on paper, use the paintbrush to apply the colours in a pleasing arrangement and use this diagram to work from.

**3** While the glass is drying, experiment with the outliner, using the shapes provided in Patterns and Templates and practising on the original grid you have painted. Use the orange outliner to make spiral shapes on all the orange squares. Keep a piece of paper towel to hand to catch any blobs. A cotton bud is also useful to lift off any mistakes! The outliner appears opaque when applied but dries clear.

## IDEAS

For a festive set of glassware try red, gold, green and white, decorated with gold and red outliners. For a stylish alternative, try dark blue, emerald green, purple and turquoise, decorated with blue and silver outliners.

**4** Use the gold outliner to fill in some more of the shapes. Allow the glassware to dry for three days before baking according to the manufacturer's instructions.

# DECORATED
## SOAP
*pump*

This is an unusual piece of glassware to

find undecorated, so buy several if you

see them. The pump mechanism is

removable so the glass may be baked.

The decorated pump would make a

perfect gift for Mother's Day, filled with

good quality liquid soap or hand cream.

Better still, why not make two and fill

them with different products? They look

wonderful wrapped in cellophane and

tied with large, wire-edged bows.

# Get ready...

GLASS SOAP DISPENSER

OVEN-BAKE GLASS PAINTS
IN EMERALD, AMARANTH
AND TURQUOISE

COMPATIBLE OUTLINERS IN
TURQUOISE, LAZULI,
EMERALD AND PEWTER

SELF-ADHESIVE
STENCIL FILM

PIECE OF SCRAP RIBBON

ADHESIVE TAPE

CLING FILM (SIRAN WRAP)

# Go!

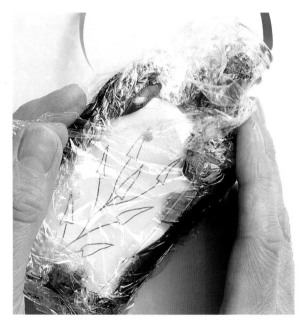

**2** Paint brushstrokes of the three paints onto the bottle, completely covering it in a blotchy pattern. Use plenty of paint for a luscious result but avoid mixing the colours together or they may become muddy.

**1** Using adhesive tape, attach a length of ribbon to the paper pattern and push it into the neck of the bottle. Fill the bottle with lentils or something similar to hold the pattern against the inside of the glass. Peel the backing off the stencil film pattern and stick it onto the front of the soap dispenser, over the paper pattern. Keep the negative part of the stencil for use on another project if you wish.

**3** While the paints are still wet, wrap the bottle in a large sheet of cling film (Siran wrap) and scrunch it onto the bottle until you like the crinkled effect it has made, then allow it to dry for about six hours. Carefully remove the cling film and leave the bottle until it is completely dry. If there are any gaps in the painting on the glass, simply paint a little colour on and dab it with scrunched-up cling film.

# Get set...

Copy the arched window design provided in Patterns and Templates onto the back of the paper-backed stencil film (see page 18 of Techniques for using stencil film) and cut out using fine scissors. Make a paper copy of the design too. Prepare the glass by washing it in hot, soapy water.

**5** Use the turquoise and lazuli outliners to add the flower heads. Work from the base of each flower by squeezing a blob of colour out and then pulling the tip away to create a fine point to each flower. It is easier to hold the bottle upside-down for this.

**4** Peel off the stencil film carefully and use a scalpel or craft knife to neaten up the edges if necessary. Now use the green outliner to draw in the stems of the flower design, keeping the tip of the nozzle clean on a piece of paper towel as you work.

**6** Use the pewter outliner to follow the edge of the arched window, adding scrolls at the top of the arch, as shown in the photograph.

Leave the bottle to dry for about a week to allow the flower heads to dry completely before baking, then follow the manufacturer's instructions for baking. To finish, fill the dispenser with white or very pale blue or green liquid soap or hand cream for a really simple, stylish gift.

# SPARKLE
## FOIL
# *mirror*

Mirrors make an ideal base for

glass painting, and the shiny metallic

and shimmering decorations that

embellish this project complement the

reflective surface beautifully. The

products chosen do not need baking

and so lend themselves perfectly to

use on mirrors.

# Get ready...

MIRROR TILE (OURS IS
30cm/12in SQUARE)

SHEET OF GLASS OR
SPARE TILE

ANTI-ADHERENT

SILVER SPARKLE GEL

SPATULA

GOLD FOIL

MOUSE MAT OR SIMILAR
SURFACE

CARD

SPRAY GLUE

OPAQUE WHITE GEL

SCALPEL OR CRAFT KNIFE

METAL RULER

WHITE SPIRIT

SILVER OUTLINER

GLOSS MEDIUM (OPTIONAL)

# Go!

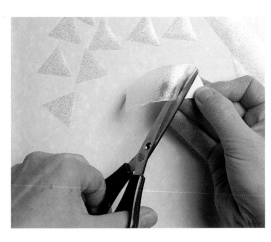

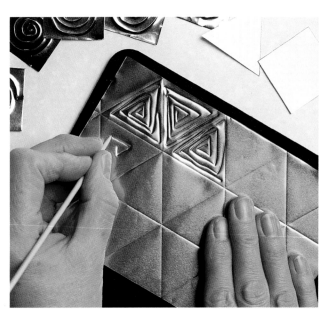

**1** Coat a sheet of glass with anti-adherent, allow it to dry, then spread some silver sparkle gel onto it using a spatula. Leave it to dry overnight and then peel it off and cut it into triangles, using the templates provided in Patterns and Templates. Put to one side.

**2** Prepare the foil pieces. As the foil is silver-backed, use both sides for a mixture of silver and gold motifs. Place the foil onto the back of a foam mouse mat or similar soft surface and then mark out a grid of squares and triangles using the template as a guide. Use a blunt pencil or knitting needle to emboss the pattern on the back of the foil. Cut out the shapes with scissors, keeping the gold and silver designs separate. Be careful as the edges can be very sharp.

**3** Carefully mask off the centre of the mirror, leaving a border of approximately 6cm (2½in) all around. Use a square of thin card to do this, stuck temporarily in the centre of the mirror with spray glue. Spread opaque white gel around the mirror using a spatula.

# Get set...

Clean the mirror tile before you start, using hot, soapy water and rinsing well. Cover your work top and wear an apron to protect your clothes.

## IDEAS

Use this design idea for any flat-sided container. It would look equally good on a glass tank or tiny, square tea-light holders. Try using coloured foils with coloured gel, perhaps pink and purple foils with green gel, or green and silver foils with blue gel and silver outliner.

**4** Gently press the foil shapes into the white gel while it is still wet (see Tip box), following your placement guide. There is no need to be too precise.

**5** Press the triangles of silver sparkle gel into any gaps that are left. Leave the card in place until the gel is completely dry (about twenty-four hours) then use a scalpel and metal ruler to cut around the card mask to reveal a perfectly straight edge. Clean the centre of the mirror with white spirit.

## TIP

It is a good idea to practise step 4 at this point and make a sketch of the foil placement before continuing, particularly if your mirror is a different size to the one used here. Removing the foil once it is placed on the gel will spoil the gel surface.

**6** With a paper towel to hand to catch any blobs, practise drawing patterns with the silver outliner on scrap paper. Draw a zigzag pattern around the foil squares, tiny dots around the foil triangles and leave the gel triangles plain. As the white gel is dry, any mistakes with the silver outliner can be removed.

Leave to dry for a full twenty-four hours. If you would prefer the gel to have a shiny finish, apply a coat of gloss medium and leave it to dry again.

# TALL
## CANDLE
# *lamp*

This is one of the few projects in the

book where a paintbrush has been

used to add the colour to the design

on the lamp shade. The interesting

patterning on the lamp base is created

using cooked spaghetti, so get planning

on cooking a spectacular spaghetti

dish for supper and start the project

afterwards. Remember to cook a little

extra and hide it before you serve!

# Get ready...

GLASS CANDLE LAMP WITH
FROSTED SHADE

COOKED SPAGHETTI

OVEN-BAKE GLASS PAINTS
IN TURQUOISE, EMERALD
AND PURPLE (WITH
OPTIONAL DILUENT)

RUBBER GLOVES

COMPATIBLE OUTLINER IN
GOLD

PAPER GLUE

CLOTHES PEGS

SOFT PAINTBRUSH

ADHESIVE TAPE

# Go!

**1** Pour some of the turquoise paint onto a plate and dip half the cooked spaghetti into it, coating it with the paint. Dab the spaghetti onto the surface of the glass lamp stand randomly, until the effect is as dense as you like. It is a good idea to wear rubber gloves for this! Leave to dry.

**2** Remove the lid from the gold outliner and squeeze some of it onto a plate (see Tip box). Take the remaining spaghetti and dip it into the gold, then over-stamp the stand with the gold colour.

**3** Make a paper pattern of the shade by wrapping it with a piece of paper and drawing around the top and base. Cut out and place it inside the shade. Mark the top and bottom where the paper overlaps and cut it to fit exactly. Open out the pattern and space the heart-shaped patterns onto it, gluing them in place with paper glue once you are happy with the spacing.

# Get set...

Cook a small amount of spaghetti, drain it, rinse it and divide into two piles. Make seven or eight copies of the pattern provided in Patterns and Templates and cut round each one. Wash the glassware.

**TIP**

Using gold outliner will give a very delicate effect. If you prefer a more spectacular gold finish, paint the whole project using solvent-based glass paints as this type of gold paint is very strongly coloured.

**4** Use clothes pegs to hold the pattern against the inside of the glass shade. Using a soft brush, paint the centre of each of the patterns with the purple paint.

**5** Continue to paint the design using the turquoise and the emerald, applying the paint with smooth brushstrokes. If you need to, add a tiny amount of diluent to make the paint flow more freely. Allow the glass to dry thoroughly.

**6** Have a piece of paper towel to hand to catch any blobs as you use the gold outliner to follow the lines of the pattern on the shade. It is easy to get flowing lines with the outliner if you lift it away from the surface of the glass and let it flow as you follow the pattern underneath. As the outliner is applied thickly using this method, allow it to dry for about a week before baking the lamp shade according to the manufacturer's instructions.

# BEAUTIFUL
## BISCUIT
*barrel*

This stunning design idea would suit

any glassware that you do not wish to

keep permanently decorated. The

technique may be adapted to suit any

occasion – from Christmas to a

children's party. The decals can be

used again and again and may be

stored when not in use, simply by

sticking them onto a sheet of plastic

or glass. They may also be used to

temporarily decorate glasses for

special occasions too.

# Get ready...

BISCUIT BARREL OR OTHER
GLASS CONTAINER

PEEL-OFF WINDOW PAINTS
IN GOLD OUTLINER AND
GOLD SPARKLE

A4 PLASTIC POCKET AND
SHEET OF PAPER

MOVABLE WORK BOARD
OR TRAY

COCKTAIL STICK

# Go!

**2** Use the gold sparkle paint to fill in the centre of the designs, using the nozzle to spread the paint into an even layer and to make sure that it touches the outline. Avoid any gaps around the edges.

**1** Using the gold peel-off outliner and holding the tube vertically, follow the outline of the designs and their details. Leave the paint to dry for several hours before moving on to the next stage as this prevents the colours from mixing accidentally.

**3** Use a cocktail stick or toothpick to draw the gold sparkle into the very narrow areas for a really neat finish.

# Get set...

It is a good idea to trace off the pattern for this project (from Patterns and Templates) several times onto a sheet of A4 paper and then slide one sheet into a plastic sleeve. Place the pattern sheet onto a tray so it can be moved later. Wash the glassware to remove all traces of grease.

**IDEAS**

How about designs featuring black cats, bats, spiders and bright orange pumpkins for a Hallowe'en party, or holly and berries for a Christmassy look?

**TIP**

Designs made from peel-off paints may be peeled and repositioned as often as you wish and can be stored on a jar. The shapes may also be stored on one side of a clear A4 pocket but do not let other peel-off shapes come into contact with them or they will stick together! Cut a sheet of card to fit inside the A4 plastic pocket in order to keep the surface firm and flat, and store the pocket in a ring binder to keep the designs safe.

SAFETY NOTE

Although peel-off paints are non-toxic, do not be tempted to decorate glassware for very small children with them as they may represent a choking hazard.

**4** Once the shapes are completely dry (see small Tip box), carefully peel them off and immediately position them onto the glass jar. Work quickly because as the shapes warm in the heat of your hand they become more malleable and difficult to handle.

**TIP**

Be patient when working with peel-off paints. Move the shapes to a level surface, well out of the way of prying fingers, for a full twenty-four hours or more if the room is very cold. If you try to remove them too soon, you may end up with a sticky mess!

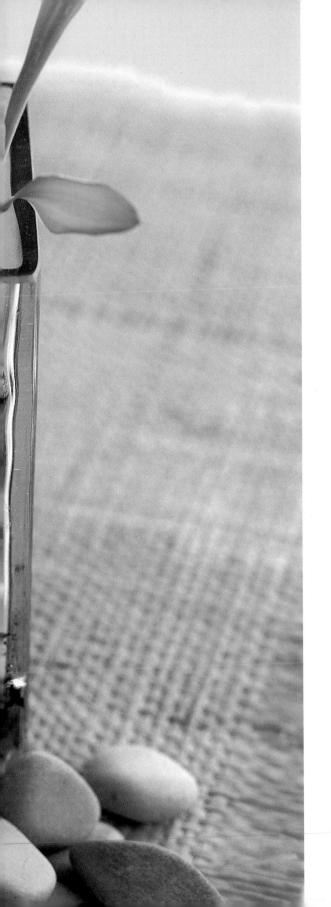

# STENCILLED
## DRAGONFLY
*tank*

This glass tank was found at a car

boot sale but they are available

commercially in a number of sizes.

Glass tanks are very easy to decorate,

particularly with stencils as they have

four flat faces to work on. Here, the

beauty of the pond side has been

captured with this lovely dragonfly

design. The shimmering wings can be

reproduced using iridescent glass

paint combined with drawing gum to

mark out the finest of veins.

# Get ready...

| | | |
|---|---|---|
| GLASS TANK | PAINTBRUSHES – SMALL AND VERY FINE | EARTH BROWN AND AMBER |
| SELF-ADHESIVE STENCIL FILM | COCKTAIL STICK | WIDE, FLAT FOAM BRUSH |
| SCALPEL | OVEN-BAKE GLASS PAINTS IN IRIDESCENT MEDIUM, SANDALWOOD GREEN, TEA GREEN, PAPRIKA, | |
| CUTTING MAT | | |
| DRAWING GUM | | |

# Go!

**1** Place the negative part of the stencil onto the glass tank, smoothing down all the edges to prevent any paint from seeping beneath it.

**2** Using a very fine brush and the drawing gum, paint in the finest of veins on the wings, using the pattern provided to guide you. This may be done freehand or alternatively tape a copy of the design inside the tank. Use as little of the gum as possible in order to produce the most delicate effect. Leave in a warm place until the gum has dried. It will become almost invisible when it has.

**3** Shake the iridescent medium thoroughly to ensure that the opalescence is well distributed in the mixture. Use a small paintbrush to apply the paint to the four wings, brushing it in the direction of the wing tips. Leave to dry.

Once the wings dry, peel off the stencil film and use a cocktail stick to pick up and remove the dried drawing gum. It should peel off the glass in one piece with any luck! Wind it onto the cocktail stick as it comes away from the glass.

# Get set...

Wash and dry the glass tank, then trace the dragonfly design (from Patterns and Templates) onto the back of the stencil film using a pencil. Lay the film onto a cutting mat and carefully cut out the design using a scalpel or craft knife.

**4** Using the small paintbrush, apply amber paint to the dragonfly head and then earth-brown stripes to the body, using the photograph to guide you.

Now paint in paprika stripes on the body, in between the amber.

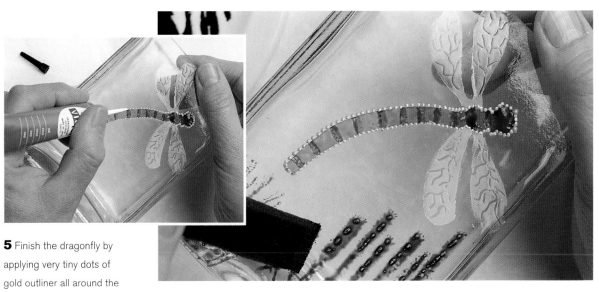

**5** Finish the dragonfly by applying very tiny dots of gold outliner all around the body and two larger dots to represent eyes.

**6** Pour out the two shades of green onto a mixing plate and dip the tip of a foam brush into the sandalwood green. Apply long, fine lines to the bottom of the tank to represent bulrushes, repeating around the sides and back of the tank. Use tea green to apply shorter strokes for the reeds, making all the lines fan out from one starting point to simulate clumps. Using a brush or very short, narrow piece of foam, paint the tops of the bulrushes using the earth brown.

Leave the tank to dry completely for several days before being tempted to bake it, following the manufacturer's instructions.

# COLOURFUL
# PATCHWORK
## *vase*

The tradition of crazy patchwork

has been copied here to make this

colourful vase. If you are feeling very

artistic and patient, each block of

colour could be painted in a number

of different ways to simulate the use

of scraps of multi-coloured fabric.

Ceramic paints have been used to

obtain a greater depth of colour as the

vase will not need frequent washing.

# Get ready...

# Go!

**2** Now apply the red paint, working just one red area at a time. (The photograph also shows one red area after it has been 'textured' with a cotton bud.)

**1** Place the prepared pattern into the vase and use a small piece of adhesive tape to hold it in place. Pour out equal quantities of the red and blue paint on a plate and mix them together to create a rich purple. Using a small paintbrush and even strokes, apply the paint in one direction according to the colour plan, if any.

**3** Use a cotton bud to immediately remove circles of red paint by dotting the bud vertically over the surface of the paint. Repeat, working on one patch of red at a time. Clean the brush with white spirit before applying the pink at random or following the colour plan.

Now mix up and apply two more colours. For the paler purple, add a little white to the first mixture you made until it becomes the right shade. For the pale blue, mix up some of the dark blue paint with white.

# Get set...

Cut a piece of paper to fit inside your vase, then copy the crazy patchwork pattern onto it (see Patterns and Templates). Join the paper into a cylinder shape using adhesive tape, making the pattern 'link up' using a pencil. You may prefer to create your own colour plan – if so, simply change the colour names within the spaces on the patchwork pattern.

**5** Add green leaves by mixing a touch of emerald green with Victoria green and using two tiny brushstrokes for each one. Once the flowers are dry, paint tiny yellow dots in the centres.

**4** Leave the vase until it has dried completely and then start on the decorations using the motifs in Patterns and Templates for guidance. Paint tiny red flowers on the pink areas using the tip of the paintbrush and working from the outer edge of each petal towards the centre.

**6** On the purple areas, paint yellow spirals with green wisps in between. Use white to paint wriggly, cross-hatched areas to the pale blue patches. Add three green dots, in groups, on the pale blue. On the mauve, paint fine six-point crosses in blue. Add a red centre to each and single red dots in the background. Finally, paint white forget-me-nots with yellow centres on the blue patches. Leave the vase to dry thoroughly.

**7** Use the pewter outliner to add the traditional style of stitching used in hand patchwork. It is a good idea to have a 'dry run' first on paper or a spare piece of glass. Try tiny crosses or rows of dots – an embroidery book will give you plenty of scope for more designs.

Finish the top edge of the vase using the outliner and leave it to dry thoroughly before use.

# TANTALIZING
## *tableware*

*This chapter features gorgeous tableware suitable for a variety of occasions and uses. Whatever the colour schemes in your home, you should be able to create your own selection of glassware to match your décor, as glass paints come in a myriad of wonderful colours.*

*You may be lucky enough to find a supplier of a glass dinner service, with a range of dinner and side plates plus matching bowls and soup dishes, enabling you to decorate your own dinner set. If the glass is painted on the back, it will be resistant to scratching from cutlery.*

# TURNTABLE
## ART
*plate*

With the advent of audio cassettes

and compact discs there is a huge

number of redundant record players

about so, if you have one, why not put

it to good use and create a plate like

this? It is great fun once you have

mastered the art, and the possibilities

are endless! The beauty of decorating

the back of a plate is that the pattern

will not be damaged by cutlery or food.

# Get ready...

| | | | |
|---|---|---|---|
| LARGE GLASS DINNER PLATE (PREFERABLY WITH NO EMBOSSED MAKER'S NAME) | SCALPEL OR CRAFT KNIFE | SPONGE | COTTON BUDS |
| | CUTTING MAT | COCKTAIL STICK | WHITE SPIRIT |
| SELF-ADHESIVE STENCIL FILM | CERAMIC PAINTS IN GOLD, NAVY, ORANGE AND YELLOW | PAINTBRUSHES – WIDE AND SMALL | |

# Go!

**1** Trace the fish design provided in Patterns and Templates onto the back of the stencil film and then cut out the shapes very carefully using a scalpel and cutting mat. Peel off the backing and position the stencil onto the back of the plate, smoothing it down well to remove any air bubbles.

**2** Using a small sponge, sponge the three fish with the gold ceramic paint, then use a cotton bud in a circular motion to remove each eye.

**3** Use a cut cocktail stick or toothpick to mark out the gills on all the fish and then leave the plate to dry overnight.

**4** Now for the fun! Lay a damp cloth on the turntable to prevent the plate slipping, then position the plate upside-down on the turntable and turn on at a slow speed to check the plate is turning evenly. If not, keep adjusting the plate until it is centralized. Turn the speed to high, load up the wide brush with plenty of navy paint, then press the brush lightly onto the centre of the plate, gradually pulling the brush towards you to create an even band of colour.

# Get set...

Remove the central spindle from your turntable; if it is non-removable, cover it with an upturned cake tin. Protect the work top and yourself from the solvent-based paints and you are ready to go. It is a good idea to practise turntable painting and a clean 'lift off' on a plain plate so you can wipe off mistakes and try again. (Refer also to Turntable Painting in Techniques page 21.)

**6** Use the small paintbrush and the gold paint (stirred well first) to make a narrow gold band that touches the navy one. Simply hold the brush in one position as the plate rotates.

**5** Use a cotton bud immediately to etch a wiggly pattern in the outer edge of the navy, pressing the cotton bud onto the paint about 2cm (1in) from the edge. Pull it towards yourself and then away from yourself – taking about a second for each forward and back movement. Lift the bud off when you feel you have etched enough pattern. It is a good idea to leave the plate on the turntable to dry before moving on to the next step.

**7** Now use the wide brush to apply plenty of the orange paint. Wipe the brush clean before dipping it into the yellow and continuing to apply paint to the plate edge.

**8** Make a simple spiral pattern by immediately holding a cotton bud on the inner edge of the orange band and slowly and steadily pulling it towards yourself. You will notice that the spiral pattern will be more pronounced the more slowly you work. Leave the plate upside-down to dry completely – this may take several days so do be patient! Ceramic paints do not need to be baked. Clean the brushes with white spirit.

# CENTREPIECE
## COMPOTE
### *dish*

This has to be my favourite project as it

is so bold and vibrant but also extremely

useful. Just imagine this huge dish

placed in the centre of a table, filled with

home-made strawberry ice-cream and

topped with tiny marshmallows. You could

even make the ice-cream while the dish

is drying! Alternatively, it would look

magnificent as a table centrepiece filled

with water and floating candles.

# Get ready...

LARGE COMPOTE DISH
OR BOWL

COMMERCIAL SPONGE-
TIPPED, LEAF-SHAPED
STAMPING TOOL (OR CUT
YOUR OWN FROM THIN FOAM)

SPONGE

FROSTED OVEN-BAKE GLASS
PAINTS IN ROSE PINK, BENGAL
PINK, MINT GREEN, ANISEED
GREEN, TEA GREEN AND CLEAR
MATT MEDIUM

COMPATIBLE OUTLINER IN GOLD

PAINTBRUSH

# Go!

**2** Add some Bengal pink to the plate and dip the sponge into this and then into the rose pink and sponge again to make the flower centres a deeper colour.

**1** Pour the rose pink paint onto a plate, then dip the sponge into the matt medium and then into the pink to make the palest shade. Wipe off any excess but be careful not to remove too much. Using the photograph as a guide, sponge the pink in large blowzy circles to create a scattering of flower heads around the dish.

**3** Pour the three shades of green onto the plate and use the foam stamp to make leaves around the flower heads. (See colour tool box page 14.) Wipe off any excess before stamping. The leaves will look more interesting if you dip into two or three of the greens for each one. Wash the foam stamp immediately after use and press it firmly onto paper towel to dry. Leave the dish until all the paint is completely dry before being tempted to carry on.

# Get set...

Wash and dry the glass as usual. If you do not have frosted paints, simply add a few drops of the matt medium to your paint colours. Experiment with mixing the colours so that you have various shades to use.

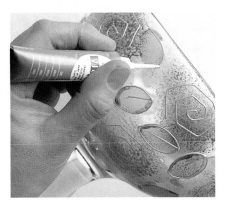

**5** Work a simple outline design detail on each of the leaves too, and then leave the dish to dry thoroughly.

**IDEAS**

Alter the design slightly by sponging some gold outliner onto the edge of the base and rim of the bowl. You could also use shades of yellow, mauve and pink for the roses for a really summery look.

**4** Use the gold outliner to create the angular spiral shapes in the centre of each rose bloom using the designs provided in Patterns and Templates to guide you. It is a good idea to try this first on a jam jar until you are happy with the result and then you can repeat the design confidently on each flower head.

**6** Sponge the stem of the dish using mint green and aniseed green. Start with the darker colour at the top and work down the stem with the paler green. Do the same for the base, using the darker green in the centre working towards a paler finish on the edge.

Leave the bowl for at least three days to dry before baking, following the manufacturer's instructions to ensure that the outliner does not bubble.

# SUNNY
## LEMON
*jug*

This sunny lemon jug conjures up images

of a hot summer day – just think of it

filled with home-made lemonade . . . mmm!

Even a complete beginner could reproduce

this design with ease. It is a very simple,

effective project to make and could also

be applied to glasses. These could either

match the jug, or be painted using other

citrus colours such as lime and orange.

# Get ready...

GLASS JUG

SELF-ADHESIVE
STENCIL FILM

MASKING TAPE

OVEN-BAKE MATT GLASS
PAINT IN LEMON

SPONGE

COMPATIBLE OVEN-BAKE
OUTLINER IN YELLOW

# Go!

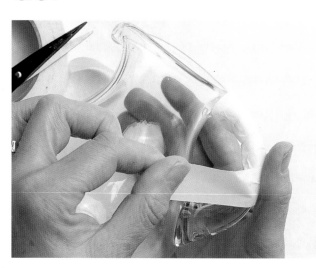

**1** Use masking tape to completely cover the handle of the jug as this will make it much easier at step 3 to produce a neat finish.

**TIP**

If there are any clear areas of glass showing once the paint has dried, simply apply a little more paint and leave to dry again. Remember that if the finished effect is bubbly or uneven it will wash off easily before it is baked. Simply cut another stencil and have another go!

**2** Position the paper pattern inside the front of the jug, using tape to hold it in place. Peel off the backing from the stencil film and stick it in place on the outside of the jug over the pattern, pressing it down hard particularly where it creases due to the curve of the glass. Do the same with the glasses if you are painting any to match.

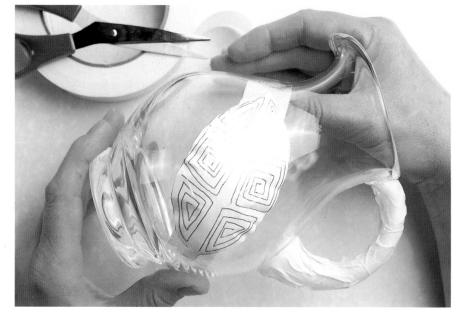

# Get set...

Prepare the glassware by washing it in hot soapy water. Make a copy of the leaf and spiral pattern from Patterns and Templates. Make a tracing of the pattern on the back of the stencil film too, and then cut it out very carefully using fine scissors so that the outer part of the stencil may be used on another project in the future, or on a large glass to match the jug.

**3** Pour a little of the lemon paint onto a saucer and then dip the sponge into it, wiping off any excess. Using a dabbing motion, sponge the paint onto the jug, working until the surface looks smooth and even. The handle is left free of paint so that it echoes the clear leaf centre. Carefully peel off the stencil (a scalpel blade works well for this) and leave the glassware until it has dried to a beautiful matt finish (see Tip box, right).

**4** Use the yellow outliner to follow the outline of the leaf and the spiral design. Have a piece of paper towel to hand to catch any blobs before you begin.

Leave the jug to dry for three full days, then bake according to the manufacturer's instructions and enjoy!

# SET
# OF TALL
# *glasses*

This is a project that you can adapt as you wish, depending upon your level of expertise. It is based on the very simple technique of using tape to mask off the areas that you do not wish to paint. You can create a set of six matching glasses, or paint each one in a different style so that everyone knows which glass is theirs.

# Get ready...

6 STRAIGHT-SIDED GLASSES

MASKING TAPE
1.5CM (½IN) WIDE

CUTTING MAT

SCALPEL

SPONGE

OVEN-BAKE FROSTED
GLASS PAINTS IN PINK,
GREEN AND PURPLE

OVEN-BAKE COMPATIBLE
OUTLINER

# Go!

**1** Cut a strip of masking tape slightly longer than the height of the glass and lay it on the cutting mat. If you are confident to cut the tape freehand, simply hold it on the mat as you begin to cut. Otherwise, transfer the design onto the tape with a pencil before you begin. For the simple wavy design, keep the knife moving as you draw it towards yourself in a flowing movement. The angled wavy line is more difficult to cut, so work slowly to create an even edge (see Tip box).

**TIP**

Angled designs are best cut in stages, lifting the blade after each straight cut. Working on a small board makes it easier to turn the board between cuts so that you are always cutting towards yourself. Use plain, uncut tape for one of the glasses.

**2** Once you have cut the masking tape in half, simply lift one half and reposition it to the side of the remaining piece so that the two straight edges of tape overlap slightly. Lift the tape and position it on the glass. Repeat with four more pieces of tape. (Use more or less strips of tape depending on the size of your project and the width of the tape being used.)

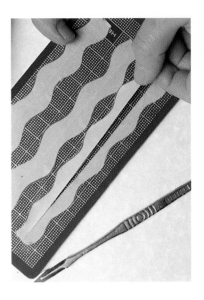

**3** Pour a little of your chosen colour onto a mixing plate, adding a little of the clear frosting medium if you want a really pale colour. Sponge the paint in the spaces between the tape and then carefully remove the tape. Leave the glasses to dry for several hours. Use a scalpel if necessary to remove any untidy edges of paint before carrying on.

# Get set...

Wash the glasses and then make a copy of the
patterned lines and the placement guide in
Patterns and Templates. Place each glass on the
guide in turn and make five small marks on the
rim using a china marker or black felt marker.

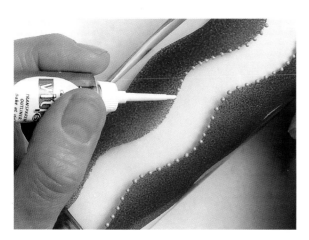

**IDEAS**

Instead of using outliner for the patterning between the
lines of masking tape, you could use felt glass painting pens.
They are available in gloss or frosted finish and are very
simple to use. Why not decorate a jug or carafe in the
same way to complete the set?

**5** Leave the finished glasses to dry for about
three days or speed the drying process by
placing them in an oven overnight at 40°C. This
will prevent the outliner from bubbling. Bake
according to the manufacturer's instructions.

**4** The spaces between the lines
of colour may be decorated using
outliner. There are several design
ideas in Patterns and Templates.
Use the outliner to edge the lines
of colour. Try tiny dots (not spaced
too close in case they merge
together), or crosses, dashes and
serrated lines. All are easier to
draw than perfectly straight lines
and will give a more contemporary
look. For best results, have a test
run of the design you intend to use,
on a jam jar or similar, practising
the shapes freehand. Alternatively,
copy the design and put it inside
the glass, holding it in place with a
paper towel. (See also Ideas box.)

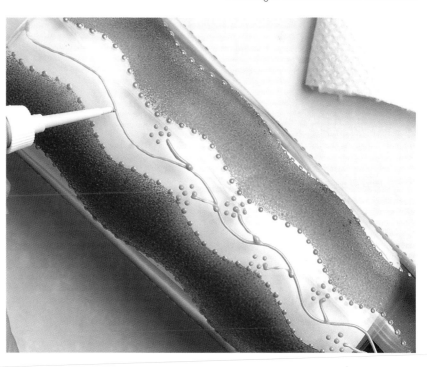

# STYLISH
# GRAPE-EDGED
# *bowl*

Grapes are perennially popular and

with the pattern provided and the

cotton bud method of painting the

grapes, you will find this project great

fun to do. The cotton bud is ideal for

painting the grapes, which look good

enough to eat! This design is perfect for

a fruit bowl, being elegant and stylish

but very easy to recreate.

# Get ready...

GLASS BOWL

SPRAY GLUE

ADHESIVE TAPE

CLOTHES PEGS

OVEN-BAKE GLASS PAINTS
IN PURPLE, ANISEED AND
EMERALD GREEN

COMPATIBLE GOLD
OUTLINER

FINE PAINTBRUSH

SPONGE

COTTON BUDS

# Go!

**2** Shake the pot of purple paint and dip a cotton bud into the lid to pick up the colour. Paint the grapes using the cotton bud in a stippling motion. You will need to use several cotton buds for all the grapes as the buds get a little woolly with constant use!

**1** Use spray glue and adhesive tape to hold the pattern on the inside of the glass, adding a few clothes pegs to secure it firmly.

**3** Pour a little of the two shades of green on a plate and mix some of each together. Using a very fine brush for the best result, start to paint the leaves using this mixture, occasionally dipping into the unmixed greens in order to create various shades. Leave the bowl until the paint has dried.

# Get set...

Wash the bowl to remove all traces of grease. Cut a
long, narrow piece of paper to fit around the bowl,
and then trace the grape design onto it (from Patterns
and Templates), repeating the pattern to the length
required. The pattern can be formed into a circle to
fit the bowl using adhesive tape.

**4** Have a practice run with the outliner
if you have never used it before and
keep a paper towel to hand to keep
the nozzle clean and catch any blobs
that appear. Outline the leaves,
allowing the outliner to flow in a wavy
line by lifting it off the glass as you
squeeze gently and follow the pattern.
Add the little stalks and tendrils. Take
care not to smudge the back of the
design as you work.

**5** When the bowl has dried completely, squeeze
some gold outliner onto the plate. Use a sponge
to dab the gold all around the base of the bowl,
applying it evenly on the base and fading out
as you approach the stem. Remove any traces
of spray glue on the inside of the bowl with
white spirit.

Leave to dry for three days before baking
according to the manufacturer's instructions.

### IDEAS

If you are copying this
design on a larger piece
of glass, the gold outliner
could be sponged
around the top too.

# SET OF
## OIL
# *bottles*

This attractive set of three bottles

came complete with a stand. The

bottles are three-sided and the backs

have been left plain to allow the

central motifs to be seen clearly.

The designs represent basil, chilli and

garlic, so why not fill the bottles with

the flavoured oils once they have

been decorated?

# Get ready...

THREE OIL BOTTLES

SPRAY GLUE

OVEN-BAKE GLASS PAINTS IN
INDIAN RED, TEA GREEN,
CLOUD WHITE AND BROWN

COTTON BUDS

SPONGE

FINE PAINTBRUSH

COCKTAIL STICK

# Go!

**1** Tear paper masks for the centre of
each bottle. This is a very rustic design
so don't be too precise when tearing.
Using spray glue, stick the masks in
place on the outside of the bottles,
making sure they are all placed at about
the same height. Shake the first pot of
paint, dip the cotton bud into the paint in
the lid and apply it to one of the bottles,
around the edges of the mask. Use the
paper mask as a guide only and do not
let the paint touch the paper or you
will lose some of the complete circles.
Repeat with the other two colours and
then let the paint dry.

**2** Remove the paper masks and then pour a little
of the first colour onto a saucer. Dip a sponge
into the paint and wipe off the excess before
sponging around the previously painted area. I
have left the necks of the bottles free of paint so
that they echo the clear centres. If you wish to do
the same, simply fade out the sponging as you
near the top. Repeat with the other two colours
and then leave the bottles to dry thoroughly.

# Get set...

This is another project where a practice run on a jam jar is a good idea. Read through the instructions and have a go at finding the right size of cotton-bud tip for the best result. (Yes, they do vary enormously!) Have a go at the painting too. Wash and dry the bottles.

**3** If you are confident to paint the motifs freehand, use a fine brush and the photograph as a guide. Alternatively, the designs provided in Patterns and Templates may be placed inside the bottles by copying them and cutting them out, leaving a long, thin paper tag poking out of the top of the bottle. The designs may be held in position against the glass by filling the bottle with lentils or small pasta pieces and pushing the stopper in place. For the red chilli, try painting it with just two strokes, then add a green tip.

**4** The basil is painted using just two brushstrokes for each leaf.

**5** The garlic is painted using the white paint. The roots are added by dipping a cocktail stick (or toothpick) into the brown paint and drawing the paint out to create the fine roots.

Remove the paper patterns, if used. Leave the bottles to dry for twenty-four hours before baking according to the manufacturer's instructions.

# DANDELION
## PASTA
### *jars*

Although this glassware was bought

as a set of pasta jars they would look

equally good filled with tea, coffee

and sugar, or even different coloured

bath salts. Dandelions always look so

pretty when they are growing in the

wild that I have worked out a way to

recreate them very simply on these

unusual jars using a foam brush,

cotton buds and outliner.

# Get ready...

SET OF THREE JARS

FOAM BRUSH 2.5cm (1in)
WIDE

SMALL PAINTBRUSH

GLASS PAINTS IN LEMON,
SAFFRON YELLOW, ANISEED
GREEN AND FROSTED
MEDIUM

COMPATIBLE PEARL WHITE
OUTLINER

COTTON BUDS

# Go!

**1** Push the pattern into each
of the jars and use pasta or
pulses to hold the paper
against the inside of the glass.
Replace the cork stoppers.

**3** The dandelion bud is
painted on the first jar with
the lemon yellow, using a fine
brush. Add a few spiky yellow
fronds to represent the
flower starting to open.

**2** Use scissors to trim the foam brush down to about
1.8cm (¾in) wide. Pour a little of the green paint for the
dandelion stems onto a saucer and have a practice run
on a piece of glass or a jam jar before starting on the
pasta jars. Dip the tip of the foam brush into the paint
and, following the pattern, use the brush to mark the
stem and the leaves, re-loading the brush occasionally.
Repeat on all three jars.

# Get set...

Wash and dry the jars. Make a paper copy of the three patterns in Patterns and Templates, using the same stem and leaves for each flowerhead. Cut to size to fit inside your jars.

**5** The dandelion clock on the third jar is painted in a different way. Use a small piece of sponge and a little of the frosted paint and sponge into a circle. Leave to dry for about half an hour before continuing.

**IDEAS**

Use the dandelion design to paint a swath of flowers on a larger piece of glass. If you use several shades of green the design will have more depth. Start with the palest green first and then work more flowers over the top. If you prefer, you could use a brush to recreate more realistically the intricate dandelion leaves.

**4** For the fully open dandelion on the second jar, use the foam brush and the lemon yellow paint and apply the colour using very close marks in a sunburst pattern.

Then take a cotton bud and immediately add texture to the centre of the flower using some of the darker saffron paint. Hold the cotton bud upright and dot it to help make the centre more realistic.

**6** Using the pearl white outliner, add some tiny crosses to represent the fluffy ends of the seed heads.

Once all three jars are painted, leave them to dry for several days, then remove the paper patterns. Ensure that the outliner has dried completely before baking according to the manufacturer's instructions.

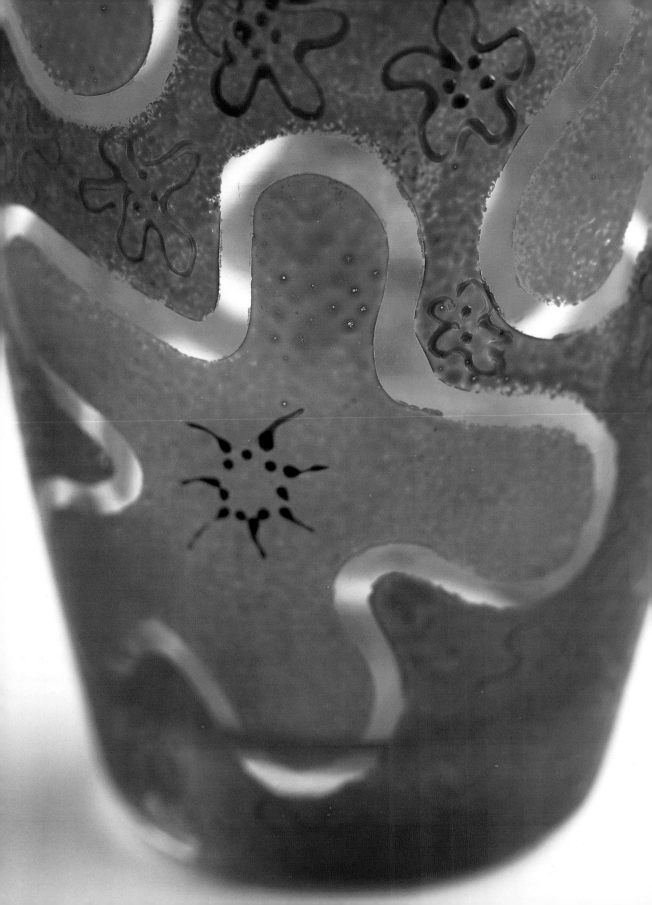

# SPARKLING
## *special occasions*

No matter what the occasion, you can decorate glassware suitably

for it and this chapter shows you how. The elegant champagne glasses

are perfect for a wedding and would be a lovely present. Christmas too

is a great excuse to decorate glass, to produce a set of baubles and a

snowman trivet to use yourself or to give away.

Hallowe'en is a fun time for children and the motifs on the mugs

may be used to decorate a matching punch bowl and serving plate too.

If you substitute peel-off glass paints for the permanent kind, you

could make some multi-occasion glassware for birthdays,

anniversaries, Easter or Thanksgiving.

# CRACKLE-
## GLAZED
# *bowl*

Here is the perfect project to make

as a centrepiece for a romantic

Valentine's dinner. When this bowl is

filled with candle-light, the delicate

crackled pattern glows beautifully. The

bowl would look equally as good filled

with dozens of pink roses. Although

the design looks complicated, it is

simply achieved by the use of crackle

glaze, a decorative paint product.

# Get ready...

GLASS BOWL

SPRAY GLUE

WIDE, FLAT PAINTBRUSH

SMALL, SOFT PAINTBRUSH

OVEN-BAKE CRACKLE GLAZE,
PHASES ONE AND TWO

COMPATIBLE MATT GLASS
PAINTS IN ANISEED GREEN,
ROSE PINK AND MINT GREEN

COMPATIBLE GOLD OUTLINER

SMALL CIRCULAR SPONGE

TINY CIRCULAR SPONGE OR
COTTON BUDS

# Go!

**1** Using spray glue or adhesive tape, fix the heart shapes randomly to the inside of the bowl until you are pleased with the spacing. Reverse half of the heart shapes to make the design more interesting.

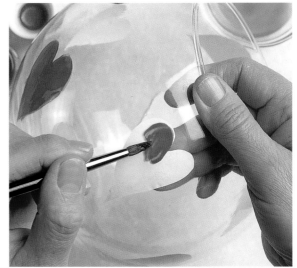

**2** Paint phase one of the crackle glaze all over the bowl using a wide, flat brush and painting in long, sweeping strokes vertically down the bowl. Be generous with the product. Allow the bowl to dry for about an hour. It will dry clear.

**3** Following the patterns beneath the glass, paint the heart shapes using the rose-pink paint and a small, soft brush.

**4** Paint the aniseed green over the rest of the bowl using the wide, flat brush. Do not overwork the paint as this may disturb the undercoat. Leave the bowl until the paint is dry.

# Get set...

Find an old jam jar to use as a practice piece for the crackle glaze technique. Read and follow the manufacturer's instructions carefully as you may be using a different crackle glaze product from ours. Wash and dry the glass bowl to remove all traces of grease. Trace or photocopy the heart design given in Patterns and Templates about eight times, cutting out the shapes.

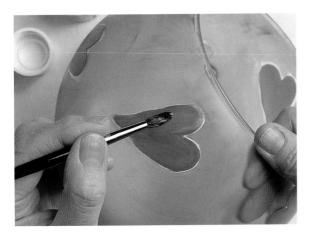

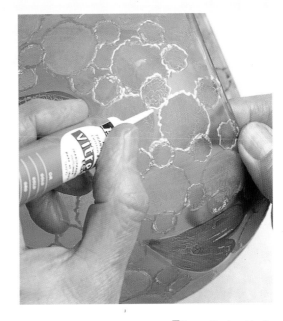

**5** Apply phase two of the crackle glaze to the hearts using the small, soft brush. Do not apply phase two to the green areas yet.

**6** For the green background crackled pattern, pour some of phase two into a saucer and then dip the small circular sponge into it and press it onto the surface of the glass. Keep reloading the sponge as necessary to make sure that the glaze is being applied generously but not dripping. Use the tiny circular sponge in the same way to fill in the spaces.

**7** Leave the bowl to dry completely for twenty-four hours. The crackle effect will reveal itself as the paint dries. The final decoration is with gold outliner, although you could omit this stage if you like the effect as it is. I have used the outliner to show how it may be used to add a little more texture and interest to the design. Have a paper towel ready to catch any blobs of outliner and then carefully trace around some of the circles using a slightly wiggly line. Leave the bowl to dry for three days to prevent the outliner from bubbling, then bake according to the manufacturer's instructions.

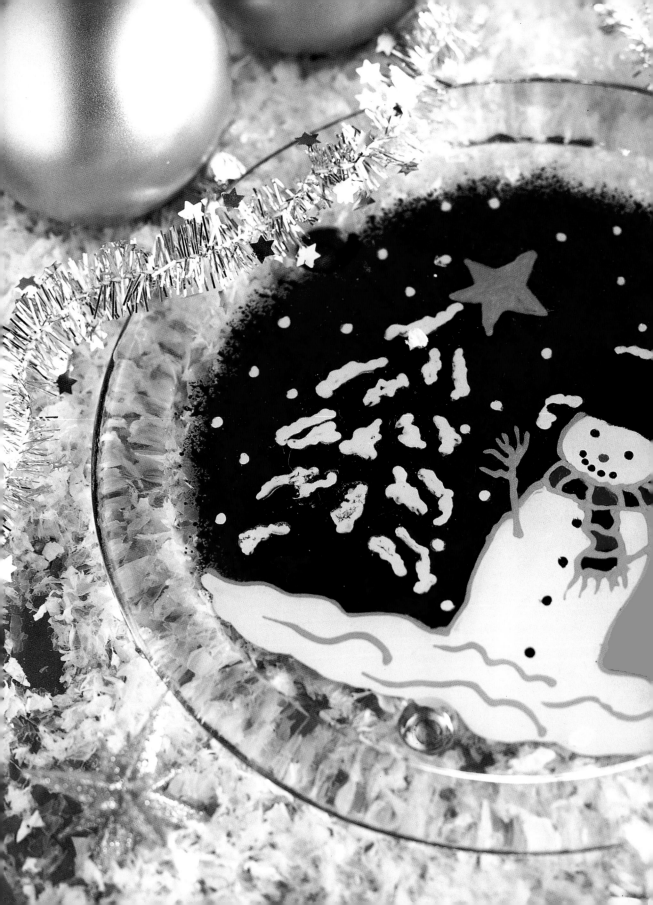

# CHARMING
## SNOWMAN
### *trivet*

This charming, festive design decorates

the back of a glass trivet and would

also work well on the back of glass

plates. If you use this technique and

incorporate words, remember to write

them in reverse! To achieve colour with

a more opaque finish, ceramic paints

have been used. These do not need to

be baked but may be hand washed

with care, and are perfect for non-food,

decorative items. The paints may be

mixed to create a huge range of colours.

# Get ready...

GLASS TRIVET ABOUT
20CM (8IN) DIAMETER

SPRAY GLUE OR
ADHESIVE TAPE

CERAMIC PAINTS IN WHITE,
DARK GREEN, NAVY BLUE
AND GARNET RED

NON-BAKE OUTLINERS IN
WHITE, BLACK AND GOLD

PAINTBRUSHES –
FINE AND MEDIUM

WHITE SPIRIT

SPONGE

# Go!

**1** Using the gold outliner, follow the outlines of the snowman, his stocking and scarf. Outline and fill in the star too. Keep a piece of paper towel to hand to keep the nozzle clean and to catch any drips.

**2** Using the black outliner, add his eyes, mouth, buttons and hat. Use the red paint and a fine brush to paint his nose. (See Tip box.)

**3** Allow the outlines to dry for an hour before using the white outliner to outline the snowman and the tree and to make the dots of snow in the sky. Add the extra snowy bits to his hat and the tree, then leave until the outliner is completely dry.

**TIP**
Keep a check on your painting by carefully turning the trivet over occasionally to check your progress.

# Get set...

Using a piece of paper and a pencil, draw round your trivet or plate and cut out the shape. Copy the snowman design from Patterns and Templates onto the paper, positioning it centrally. Make sure the glassware is clean and dry and then tape the pattern onto the front of the trivet. Alternatively, hold it flat against the glass using spray glue.

**4** Use a medium brush to paint the tree using the dark green ceramic paint, painting over the white snowy areas. Paint the scarf and stocking with the dark green and garnet red ceramic paints alternately, using the finer brush. Leave until thoroughly dry to prevent any colour running at the next step.

**5** Use the white paint for the ground and then fill in the snowman's body, painting over his features and buttons. Leave to dry for a few hours and then repeat, ensuring that the white paint is sufficiently dense.

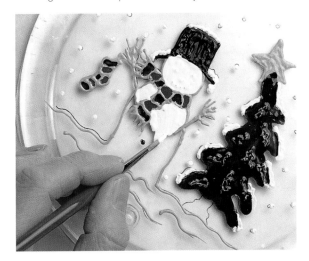

**6** Once the white paint is dry, sponge the navy blue over the back of the whole trivet leaving a roughly sponged edge all around.

Leave it to dry upside-down for several days. Remove the paper pattern and any glue residue (if used) with a little white spirit.

# ELEGANT
## CHAMPAGNE
## *flutes*

These elegant champagne glasses

are simple to decorate and would be

perfect for a summer wedding. The

design has three variations – one

vertical, one horizontal and one

meandering – all equally stylish. This

is another project that allows you to

choose one or more design ideas

along the same theme. You could

even make a matching canapé plate

by painting the back of a clear glass

plate in the same pattern.

# Get ready...

6 CHAMPAGNE FLUTES

SOFT, DARK FABRIC

OVEN-BAKE, FROSTED,
COLOURLESS, FELT GLASS
PAINTING PEN

OVEN-BAKE GOLD
OUTLINER

VERY NARROW
MASKING TAPE

# Go!

**2** Using the gold outliner,
add gold dots to the base of
some of the leaves. Work
very freely to keep the design
fresh, and try to keep the
dots really small and neat.

**1** FOR THE VERTICAL DESIGN
Begin by positioning a
glass upside-down on the
placement guide provided on
page 119 of Patterns and
Templates. Make five tiny
marks on the rim of the glass
using the felt glass painting
pen. Following the vertical
leafy design provided in
Patterns and Templates, use
the pen to draw curvy lines
vertically down the glass,
making the line straighter as
you work down the stem. Add
the leaves, staggering them
down the stems.

**3** FOR THE HORIZONTAL DESIGN
Use the same pattern as before
but draw the wavy lines around
one of the glasses in bands.
You may find the spacing easier
if you mask off the glass using
very narrow masking tape,
available in art shops. Draw the
wavy line above the tape or
band and then remove the
tape. Add the leaves and gold
outliner as before.

# Get set...

Prepare the felt pen by shaking it thoroughly and depressing the tip on a hard surface. If using a new pen, do this for at least thirty seconds as it takes a while for the paint to come through. Wash and dry the glasses. Find some soft, dark fabric to push inside the glasses to make it easier to see the design as you work.

**4** FOR THE MEANDERING DESIGN Use the pattern provided in Patterns and Templates as a guide, drawing the design freehand onto a glass. If you are not confident to work directly on the glass, try copying the pattern onto paper, tracing the design over and over until you are more confident. Outline the long, curvy lines first and then add the leaf shapes, staggering them and filling any large gaps with them. Allow the glass to dry before moving on.

**5** Decorate the base of each of the glasses by drawing a wavy line around each one with gold outliner and adding leaves and gold dots to match the glasses.

Allow the glasses to dry for three days before baking according to the manufacturer's instructions.

**IDEAS**

If the champagne glasses are for a wedding, you could create designs featuring horseshoes, bows and flowers. For Christmas, use motifs featuring fir trees, holly, mistletoe or bows. Other design ideas include using squares, triangles, dots and squiggles. For New Year, make a feature of the date.

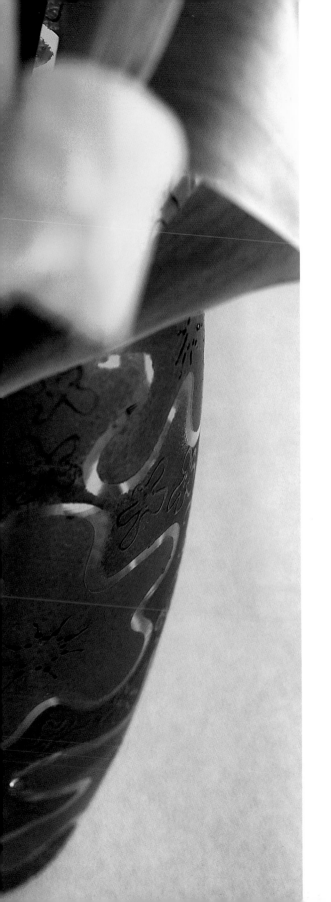

# BLUE
## SPLAT
*vase*

The 'splat' design on this tall vase is

amazingly simple to copy and produces

a dramatic effect. As peel-off window

paint has been used to create the

stencils for the shapes, the project

takes a few days to complete. However,

if you are confident to work directly

onto glass, and especially if your glass

item is flat-sided, you could use

masking fluid to mask off the shapes,

instead of the peel-off paint.

# Get ready...

TALL VASE

A4 PLASTIC POCKETS

PEEL-OFF WINDOW PAINT
OUTLINER

OVEN-BAKE FROSTED GLASS
PAINTS IN AZURE BLUE AND

GITANE BLUE

COMPATIBLE OVEN-BAKE
OUTLINERS IN BLACK AND
TURQUOISE

SPONGE

COTTON BUDS

TINY SPONGE DOT
APPLICATOR (OR MAKE
YOUR OWN)

# Go!

**1** Make the peel-off stencils using the window paint outliner (see also Techniques page 18). You can use it in the same way as icing – simply hold it above the plastic sleeve and allow it to flow freely from the tube, following the contours of the design within the sleeve. Once complete, leave flat in a safe place to dry for twenty-four hours, well out of the reach of children and cats!

**2** Peel off one shape at a time and place onto the clean vase, spacing them evenly as you go. The shapes are quite tricky to handle if the room is very warm. If you have any trouble, simply pop them in the freezer for a few minutes to firm up!

**3** Pour a little of the azure blue paint onto a mixing plate and sponge this into the centres of each of the shapes. This is when the little sponge dot applicator is useful for getting into the tight corners of the design (see Tip box).

# Get set...

Copy the large splat design from Patterns and Templates onto a sheet of paper (about six times per sheet). The total number of splats you need will depend on the size of vase you are using – the one shown needed eight. Slide one of the sheets of paper into a plastic sleeve.

**5** The smaller splat pattern (see Patterns and Templates) adds further detail to the vase but it is a good idea to practise drawing these shapes freehand on paper in a variety of sizes before moving on.

**4** Now use the darker gitane blue to sponge around the shapes, making sure you work right up to the edge of the stencil for a really sharp finish. Use a moistened cotton bud to remove any paint that strays over the lines. Peel off the shapes by using the tip of a cocktail stick and then use a scalpel to neaten any edges if necessary. Allow the vase to dry thoroughly.

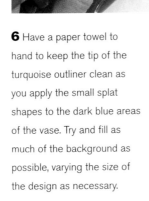

**6** Have a paper towel to hand to keep the tip of the turquoise outliner clean as you apply the small splat shapes to the dark blue areas of the vase. Try and fill as much of the background as possible, varying the size of the design as necessary.

**7** Finish the design by adding more decoration to the centres of each pale blue shape with black outliner as shown. Leave the vase to dry for at least three days before baking according to the manufacturer's instructions.

# DELICATE
## CHRISTMAS
*baubles*

These delightful, clear-glass baubles

were just begging to be painted!

I chose to use ceramic paints on them

as the colours are strong and opaque

and the baubles do not need to be

baked once decorated. The designs

shown are simple to recreate freehand

and all use the same techniques, with

the holly design described fully first.

# Get ready...

CLEAR-GLASS BAUBLES

TACKY RE-USABLE PUTTY

MUG

CERAMIC PAINTS IN RED
AND TWO SHADES OF GREEN

FINE PAINTBRUSH

WHITE SPIRIT

NON-BAKE OUTLINER IN
GOLD

TRACING PAPER

# Go!

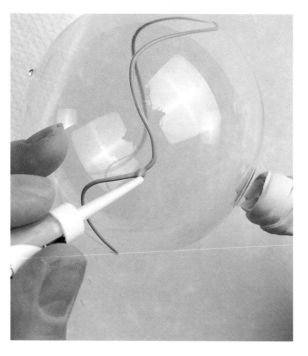

**1** Remove the wire gently from the bauble, taking care, as the neck of the bauble is very delicate. Wrap a pencil with a little of the tacky putty and push it into the top of the bauble. Wrap a little more putty around the neck of the bauble and the pencil to hold them secure. Use a mug to stand the painted bauble in.

**2** FOR THE HOLLY DESIGN
Holding the bauble horizontally and using the gold outliner, squeeze a wavy trail onto the bauble as you rotate it with the other hand. Try to get the end to meet up with the beginning! If you have trouble judging this, simply place an elastic band around the glass in a wavy fashion and apply the outliner nearest the neck end of the bauble. Remove the band before proceeding.

**3** Using the outliner (and the photograph to guide you), add the next part of your chosen design to create the stems and leaves.

# Get set...

Copy out the designs provided in Patterns and Templates by tracing them directly onto tracing paper. Cover the tracing with a sheet of clear glass and use this to practise on before tackling the baubles.

**IDEAS**

Use wide, wire-edged ribbon in gold to tie the baubles to the Christmas tree, or make your own festive decoration by spraying some branches with gold acrylic spray. Alternatively, hang the baubles with lengths of invisible thread or fine ribbon.

**4** Pour out a little of each of the two green paints onto a mixing plate and blend them loosely together. Paint the green holly leaves using the fine brush – painting the outline first and then carefully filling in each leaf.

**FOR THE FOUR OTHER DESIGNS**

Follow the designs given in Patterns and Templates and repeat steps 1–5 above, varying the red-painted areas according to the individual patterns. All the leaves, both large and small, are painted using two brushstrokes, brushing towards the tip. To paint the daisy flowers, start from the tips and pull the brush towards the centre. Paint the tulip flowers with three brushstrokes – starting with the central one brushing up to the tip, then adding one petal on either side. For the elongated heart design, paint the curved outline first, fill in and then brush towards the tip. For the design with seven tiny red flowers, paint one brushstroke from the base to the tip for each little flower.

**5** Shake the red paint very well and use the fine brush to paint the holly berries, varying the number of berries for each group of holly leaves. When you've finished, clean the brush in white spirit and dry with paper towel.

Stand the bauble in the mug until dry. Replace the hanging wire by squeezing the two prongs together before pushing it into the neck of the bauble. It is advisable to leave the bauble in the air for several days before being tempted to pack it in a box.

# SPECIAL
# CELEBRATION
## *jar*

This magnificent, cork-stoppered

apothecary jar was just begging to

be decorated and the idea may be

adapted to suit similar occasions.

This one is to celebrate a ruby wedding

anniversary but it would be equally

suitable for a silver (twenty-five years)

or golden (fifty years) anniversary, or

an eighteenth or twenty-first birthday.

Numbers have been supplied in

Patterns and Templates, so all you

have to do is change the colouring

to suit the occasion.

# Get ready...

LARGE APOTHECARY JAR

A4 PAPER AND PLASTIC
SLEEVE

PEEL-OFF WINDOW PAINT
OUTLINER

SELF-ADHESIVE STENCIL
FILM

SCALPEL

CUTTING MAT

OVEN-BAKE GLASS PAINTS IN
INDIAN RED AND TEA GREEN

COMPATIBLE OVEN-BAKE
OUTLINER IN PEWTER

SPONGE

DRESSMAKER'S WATER-
VANISHING BLUE FELT PEN

FINE PAINTBRUSH

**TIP**

The stencil may be
re-used many times.
Simply place it onto a
sheet of glass or mirror
to hold it flat as you wash
it under cool water.

# Go!

**1** Holding the tube of
window paint outliner almost
vertical, follow the lines of the
diamond grid, allowing the
glass paint to flow out freely
by holding it slightly above the
surface as if piping icing. Set
the stencil aside to dry for a
full twenty-hours!

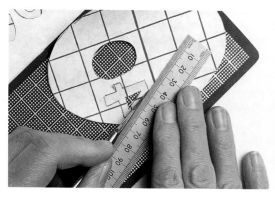

**2** Meanwhile, you can make the oval stencil. Lay the paper-
backed stencil film over the oval pattern (supplied in Patterns
and Templates) and copy it very carefully. If you wish to include
numbers in your design, copy them too, making sure that they
are *in reverse*. Lay the stencil film onto a cutting mat and carefully
cut out the oval with a scalpel. Cut out the numbers too. For
numbers with straight sides it is a good idea to use a metal ruler
to cut against for a really neat result. Keep the tiny centres of the
numbers as they will be needed.

**3** Peel the paper backing off
the stencil film and position
the oval stencil onto the jar.
Replace the centres of the
numbers too and press down
all the edges firmly.

**4** When the diamond grid
stencil is completely dry, peel
it off the plastic A4 sheet and
position it on the jar, covering
the oval pattern. Pour some
of the red paint onto a saucer
and dip the sponge into it,
wiping off any excess.
Sponge the gaps in the grid
and around the oval stencil.
Lift off the diamond stencil.

# Get set...

Wash the glassware and dry thoroughly. Draw a diamond grid on A4 paper spacing the lines 2.5cm (1in) apart (see Patterns and Templates). It is a good idea to wrap the paper around your jar and cut it to the size you want to make your stencil. Place the paper pattern into the plastic sleeve and lay it on a tray or similar surface that may be moved while the stencil is drying.

**5** Sponge the numbers using the same red paint. Leave until dry before being tempted to remove the stencil film. Use the tip of a scalpel to remove the centres of both numbers.

**6** Use the blue felt pen to draw the branch of the flower design, adding a few sprigs for leaves. Go over this using the pewter outliner. Have a paper towel handy to keep the tip of the nozzle clean and to catch any blobs.

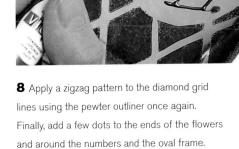

**7** Paint the flowers using a fine paintbrush and the red paint. Work outwards towards the tip of each petal using single brushstrokes. Add the leaves using the green paint, making just one brushstroke from the sprig outwards.

**8** Apply a zigzag pattern to the diamond grid lines using the pewter outliner once again. Finally, add a few dots to the ends of the flowers and around the numbers and the oval frame.

Leave the jar to dry thoroughly for several days. Remove the cork before baking according to the manufacturer's instructions.

# HALLOWE'EN
## PARTY
## *mugs*

Hallowe'en parties are such fun,

and hot apple and cinnamon is a

wonderfully warming drink to serve

at them. These mugs would make

great gifts for children to take home

afterwards. As an alternative to

decorating mugs, use the same

design on tall, straight-sided glasses

if you plan to serve cold drinks. You

could even make a matching punch

bowl using all the designs repeated

around the outside.

# Get ready...

GLASS MUGS

NARROW MASKING TAPE

MASKING TAPE FOR CURVES

STENCIL FILM

SCALPEL

CUTTING MAT

SPONGE

OVEN-BAKE GLASS PAINTS IN
PAPRIKA ORANGE, TEA
GREEN, FROSTED WHITE,
BLACK AND CLEAR MATT
MEDIUM

COMPATIBLE OUTLINER IN
PEWTER AND PEARL WHITE

FINE PAINTBRUSH

COTTON BUDS

# Go!

**1** Prepare the stencil for the mugs. Copy each of the designs from Patterns and Templates onto the back of the paper-backed stencil film and then place them onto a cutting mat and cut out neatly using a scalpel. (A new blade makes precision cutting so much easier!) Cut out the features from the pumpkin and keep them safe as they will be needed later.

**2** Peel off the paper backing and position the stencils onto the mugs. Begin sponging the bat (or other designs) as described in the box (right).

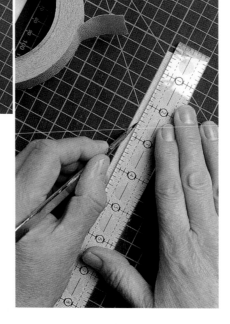

**3** Lay a length of the masking tape for curves onto the cutting board, lining it up with the board markings to make sure it is straight, and then use the scalpel and ruler to cut 5mm (¼in) strips from it (see Tip box). Take the cut strips and place them onto each mug, top and bottom, in a wavy line all round. Press the tape down firmly to prevent the paint seeping beneath it.

**TIP**

If you do not have any masking tape for curves, use wide elastic bands instead.

# Get set...

Wash the mugs and dry them thoroughly. If your mugs have chrome areas (these were from Habitat), then mask these areas off using narrow masking tape. Alternatively, remove the chrome handle if possible.

## STENCIL DESIGNS

### BAT DESIGN

Pour a little of the black paint onto a mixing plate and add a little matt medium to it. Mix well and then sponge the bat shape. Remove the stencil.

### PUMPKIN DESIGN

Mix equal quantities of the orange and frosted white paint together, making enough of this mixture for the tops and bottoms of all the mugs as well as the pumpkin motif. Carefully sponge on the pumpkin shape. Add a green stalk and use the black paint and a fine brush to paint the features. Finally, use the orange paint (neat) to paint in the fine vertical stripes.

### GHOST DESIGN

Use frosted white, which is then outlined with the pearl white outliner. Use tiny dots of the pewter outliner for his eyes.

**4** Using the orange and frosted white paint mix, sponge around all the mugs, working the paint until the effect is very fine and even. Peel off the masking tape once the paint is dry and use a scalpel to remove any paint that has strayed beneath it. Alternatively, if you remove the tape while the paint is still wet, a cotton bud may be used to clean up any rough edges.

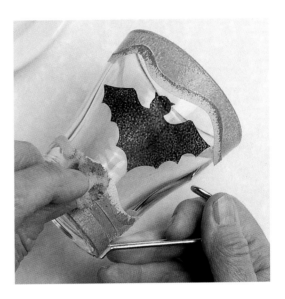

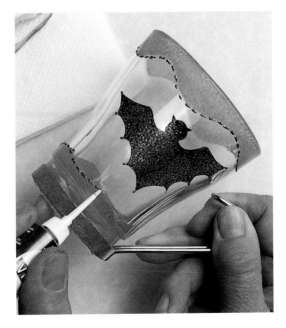

**5** Use the pewter outliner to add tiny dashes all around the edge of the curvy orange bands on the mugs. Use it to add eyes to the ghost too. Keep a piece of paper towel close to hand to keep the nozzle clean as you work.

Leave the mugs to dry thoroughly for several days before baking according to the manufacturer's instructions. Meanwhile, get busy sending out those invitations!

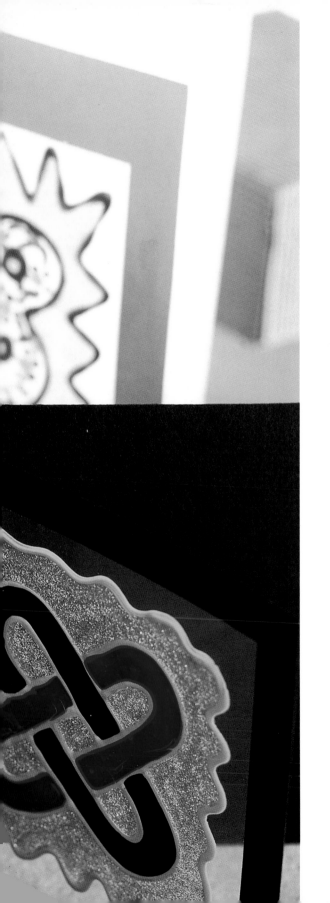

# PEEL-OFF
## GIFT
*Cards*

Here is an 'apeeling' idea to create

a greetings card and small gift all

in one. There is a choice of three

designs – a Chinese character

meaning life, a simple Celtic knot

pattern and an eighteenth birthday

motif. Peel-off window paints have

been used so the motifs adhere

temporarily to the acetate windows

on the cards. The motifs may then

be peeled off and repositioned onto

any shiny surface such as a mirror,

window or fridge door.

# Get ready...

PEEL-OFF WINDOW PAINTS
IN GOLD AND BLACK
OUTLINERS

PEEL-OFF WINDOW PAINT IN
RED (ADDITIONAL COLOURS
IN YELLOW, DARK GREEN,

RAINBOW SPARKLES, GOLD
SPARKLES AND CLEAR)

A4 PLASTIC SLEEVE

A4 BLACK CARD

SCALPEL

METAL RULER

DOUBLE-SIDED TAPE

ACETATE 14.5 X 15CM
(5¾ X 6IN)

# Go!

**1** Using the black outliner and holding the tube
vertically, follow the lines of the design allowing the
black paint to flow out. Fill in each section of the
design as you go.

**2** Now outline the outer
edge of the design using
the gold outliner. Keep a
paper towel to hand to
keep the nozzle clean.

**3** Fill in the spaces
between the characters
and the edge with the
red paint. You will find
the easiest way is to
allow the paint to flow
against the edge of the
painted motif and edging
and then allow the
remaining area to fill in
with the red paint.

**4** Once the motif is finished, you may notice a few
tiny air bubbles in the paint. If so, use a cocktail stick
or a pin to prick them before the product has been
allowed to dry. Place the motif flat in a safe place to
dry for at least twenty-four hours.

# Get set...

Copy the design provided in Patterns and Templates onto a sheet of A4 paper and slide it into an A4 plastic sleeve.

**TIP**

If you prefer, you could work the designs straight onto the acetate window but it is more difficult to remove the peel-off paint from this surface. Make sure that the recipient of the card knows that the motif may be peeled off and repositioned onto a window, mirror or fridge door.

**5** While the motif is drying, you can make the window card. Fold a sheet of black A4 card in half, creasing it accurately. Open it out and place it onto a cutting mat. Use a pencil to mark out a window 10cm (4in) square and then cut it out using a scalpel and metal ruler for a really neat finish.

**6** Cut double-sided tape to size and press it onto the card, as close to the edge of the window as possible. Peel off the backing and then press the acetate onto it. Be accurate – it is impossible to peel it off and start again!

## CARD DESIGNS

### CELTIC DESIGN
Outline the pattern as above but fill in with the red and green paints. The background of the design is filled in with the gold sparkle paint.

### '18' DESIGN
Start by making tiny red dots for the flowers and leave to dry. Then add yellow dots in the centres and green stalks and leaves. Once again, leave the paint to dry. Outline the numbers with gold and then use clear paint to fill in the centre of the numbers. It is all right to allow the paint to obscure the flowers as it will eventually dry clear. Finally, outline the design with the gold outliner and fill in with the rainbow sparkle. Fill in the centres of the number 8 too.

**7** Peel off the motif and position it centrally over the acetate window on the gift card. You will notice how the colours change from being milky when wet to clear once they are dry.

# PATTERNS AND TEMPLATES

The patterns and templates supplied on the following pages are
the motifs you will need for the projects. They have been
produced actual size so you can trace or photocopy them. Most
of the motifs are very simple shapes, so many of you
will be able to draw them easily freehand if you prefer.

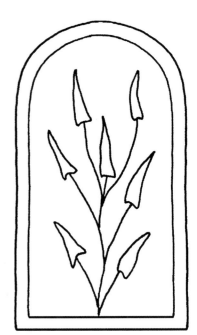

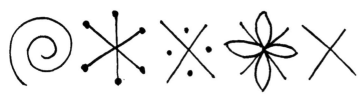

Set of candle holders  p24

Decorated soap pump  p28

Sparkle foil mirror  p32

Tall candle lamp  p36

Beautiful biscuit barrel  p40

Turntable art plate p54

Stencilled dragonfly tank p44

Centrepiece compote dish p58

Sunny lemon jug p62

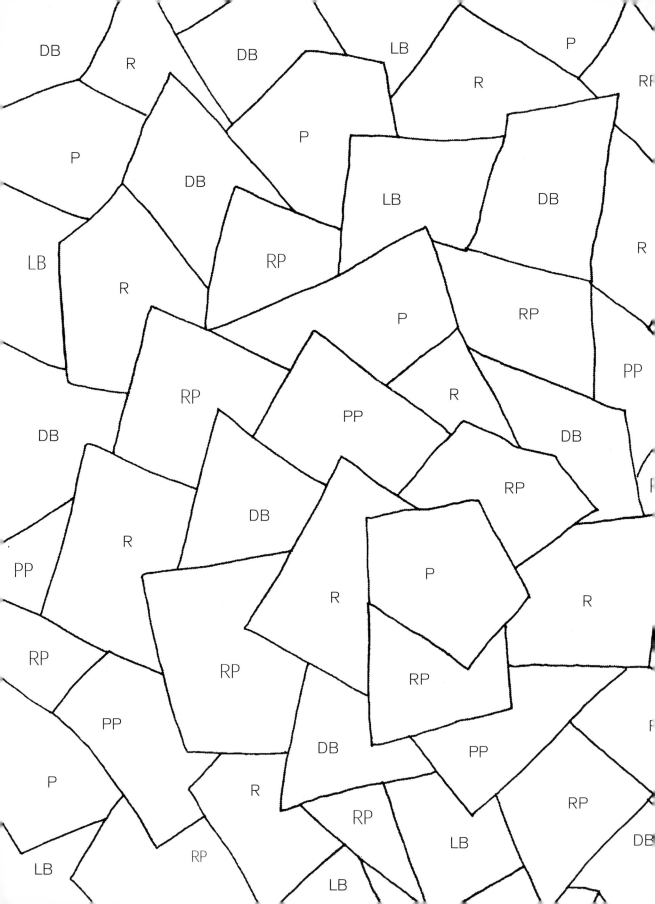

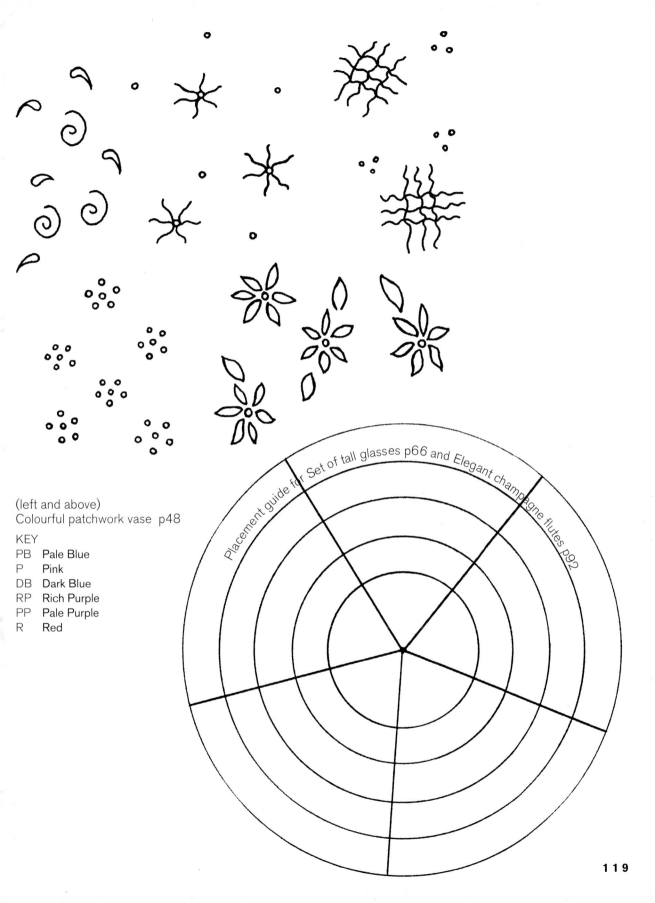

(left and above)
Colourful patchwork vase  p48

KEY
PB  Pale Blue
P   Pink
DB  Dark Blue
RP  Rich Purple
PP  Pale Purple
R   Red

Placement guide for Set of tall glasses p66 and Elegant champagne flutes p92

Masking tape cutting shapes for Set of tall glasses  p66
(see placement grid on p119)

Set of tall glasses patterns

Stylish grape-edged bowl  p70

Dandelion pasta jars  p78
(use the same stem and
leaves pattern for all three
types of flowerhead)

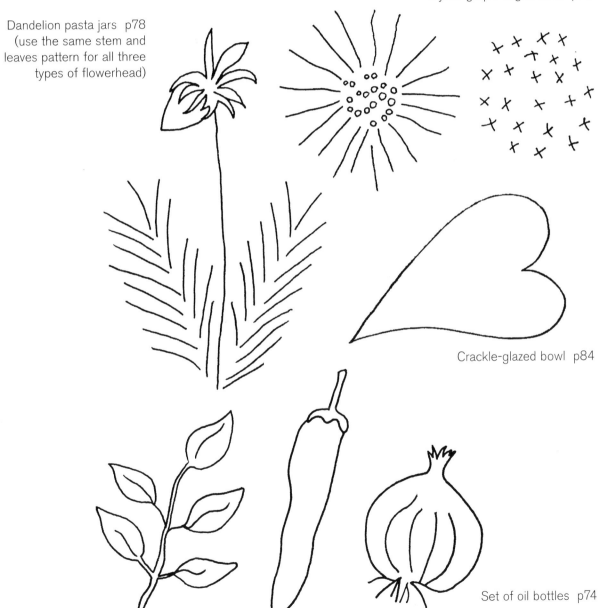

Crackle-glazed bowl  p84

Set of oil bottles  p74

Charming snowman trivet  p88

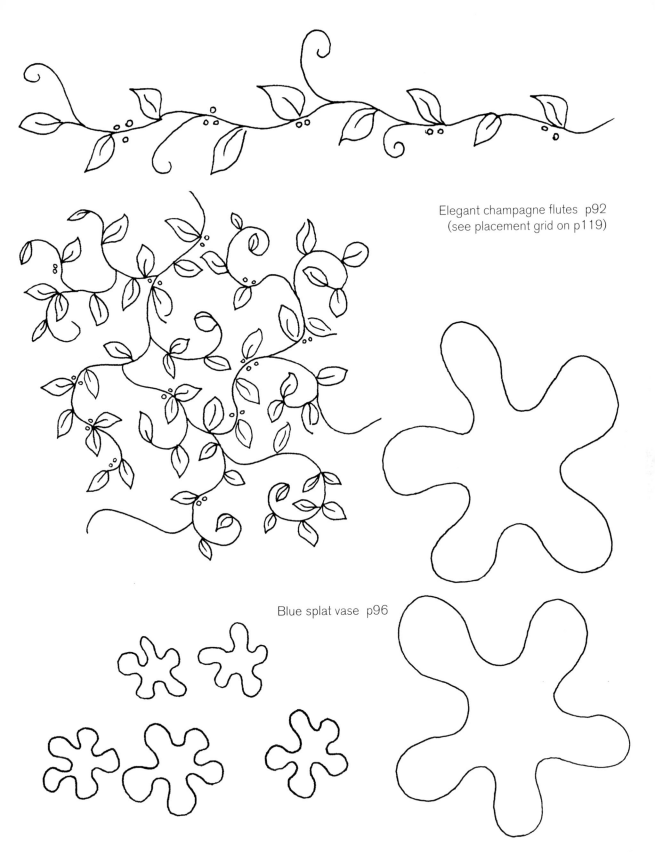

Elegant champagne flutes p92
(see placement grid on p119)

Blue splat vase p96

Delicate Christmas baubles  p100

Hallowe'en party mugs  p108

Special celebration jar and numbers  p104

Peel—off gift cards p112

# Suppliers

For general British stores stocking a variety of glassware, try Focus Do It All (for soap pump), Debenhams, Habitat and other large department stores.

## Clearcraft
Unit 1
Estate Way
London
E10 7JN
tel: 020 8556 5112
fax: 020 8539 9015
email: Clearcraft@aol.com
website: www.clearcraftltd.co.uk
*Range of glassware, including
candle holders and candle lamp*

## Pébéo UK Ltd
109 Solent Business Centre
Millbrook Road West
Millbrook
Southampton
SO15 0HW
tel: 02380 701144
email: pebeo@aol.com
website: www.pebeo.com
*Details of local stockists of Pébéo products*

## Rainbow Silks
6 Wheeler's Yard
High Street
Great Missenden
Bucks
HP16 0AL
tel: 01494 862111
fax: 01494 862651
email: caroline@rainbowsilks.co.uk
*Pébéo products via mail order*

## Woodware Toys and Gifts
Unit 2A
Sandylands Business Park
Skipton
North Yorkshire
BD23 2DE
tel: 01756 700024
fax: 01756 701097
email: sales@woodware.co.uk
*Heat-impressed foam and
stamping tools*

# Acknowledgments

I would like to thank John Wright from Pébéo for so generously supplying all the products used in this book and Clearcraft for supplying some interesting pieces of glassware. Special thanks to Tony for doing the step photography at some unearthly hour and with such patience! Thanks too to Jenny, Ali and Lin for their support and to Amanda for her delightful photographs.

# Index

Templates in *italic*